Healing Rhymes for Human Kind

A Poetic Guide for the Sensitive Soul

AngelGlow Publishing

www.TootsieRose.biz/angelglowpublishing.html

Healing Rhymes for Human Kind © 2020 Connie F. Prince

All rights reserved. No part of this book may be reproduced in any form or by any electronic or mechanical means, including information storage and retrieval systems, without written permission from the author, except in the case of a reviewer, who may quote brief passages embodied in critical articles or in a review.

Published by AngelGlow Publishing

Graphics, Editing and Layout by Bobby Prince

ISBN: 978-1-7356203-7-4

Introduction

The Reason for This Book:

In my Lifelong Journey as a Sensitive Performer wearing many unexpected 'Hats' along the way, I became more and more Intrigued with the effect one's Presence could have on another. The Feelings and Differences we could possibly make connecting with one another took the focus of my Soul's Purpose. I became more excited about the Spiritual Revelations I was receiving. My life became a voracious study of Creative Spirits and how they kept their Spiritual Center and Sanity in a world that appeared often frightening and threatening to sensitive souls like me.

After growing up with Visions Of Grandeur in my long journey through struggles and joys, I discovered it really makes no difference in the end what particular job or position we have had in this world. It is the Lessons and Growth In our Souls -- and just how Kind and Loving we have been to each other along the way -- that is The Most Important.

I am reminded of Amazing Maya Angelou's quote:

"I've learned that people will forget what you said,
people will forget what you did, but people will never
forget how you made them feel."

Our Personal Energy Profoundly Affects Those Around Us, eventually spreading one by one around the World and Universe. Perhaps that's how we can Change it -- "Let there Be Peace on Earth, and let it begin with me ...."

It is my Personal Prayer that the Words In this Poetic Offering become a Heart Handbook for your Soul, as no Soul takes this Journey Alone. Our Angels are Always just a Thought Away To Comfort Us with Spiritual Salve for our Souls.

May these Rhymes in time, bring such Comfort to Yours.

Soulfully Yours,
Connie Freeman Prince

Dedication

This Book, from the Depths Of my Soul, is Dedicated to the Heart and Soul of You -- The One Who is Reading This At This Very Moment. It is no accident these Poems have found their way to You, as it was my Destiny they also found me. It is my Deepest Prayer they bring you Comfort, Peace, and Soul Inspiration on your Personal Path To Enlightenment. I am Grateful and Honored our Spirits have crossed on this Page of Life. May Angels' Wings Surround and Embrace You and Your Precious Child Within on your Ever Evolving Journey Through this Magical Life! I Thank You from the Depths of my Heart and Soul for being part of mine.

In the Breath Of Divine Love,
Connie Freeman Prince

This Life is a Rhyme
Of All Humankind
A Mixture of Verses
A Measure of Time...

That helps us to Focus
On Beauty and Truth
Life's Mystery Shows Us
The Poetic in You!

Ways to Experience this Book

• "Poem Menu" (next page) --
> Move your Fingers upon the "Menu"
> And See Where e'er they Stop.
> It's your Message for the Day --
> From your Angels: Thoughts to Shop :-)

• Acknowledge an Emotion you're feeling and find a corresponding Listing in the Index (Page 348) to hopefully lead you to a Poem with a Special Message for you.

• Get Quiet, Breathe Deeply and Ask Your Angels for your 'Message' for the day .... Shuffle the pages and let the Book Fall Open to the Poem you're meant to read at this time. The Message in the Poem you fall upon is for You.

• Just Begin from The Beginning -- always a Sweet Place To Start.

Love and Inspired Blessings To Your Journey!

Thank You for sharing these moments of your life with my words. I respect how Valuable and Irreplaceable your Time spent 'away from the bustling outside world' Is.

It is an honor you have chosen to rest a spell with my humble heart and soul ponderings and revelations.

I am Grateful to our Great Creator who sent them through me -- To You!

A Poem Of Preface

Poems for your Journey
Salve for your Soul
Especially when stubbing a 'Spiritual Toe'...
I pray these Rhymes Inspire your Time
On This Road we are Traveling
Hand in Hand, Angels Kind.

Table of Contents

Poem Menu

"My Life In Rhyme"

*Poems for the Sensitive Spirit Surviving
in an Ego Driven World.*

"Spirit Star Search"

Once Upon a star lit night
On the Planet Ego Earth,
There lived an Inspired Artist
Who dreamed of Fame unheard.

She rehearsed her trek to Stardom
From infancy remembered
Songs and Parts and Ways to Shine
Her Light still Unencumbered.

But as she grew so did her thirst
For knowledge of How stars shine
Just shining without meaning
Seemed so shallow she would find.

She got more satisfaction
From the study of their Souls
Combined with Heart Reactions
Of others fed her goal.

Then after years of thinking
She Really Wanted to Dance
Her Light across the Galaxies,
She kept praying for The Chance.

But each time she would get oh so close
To the Star Shine that she dreamed,
Detours of the Soul appeared
That needed help it seemed.

So she shined her Light as Bright as she could
For these unexpected turns,
All the while her mind would burn
Thinking "Is This The Path I earned?"

I always thought my Value lay
In what the Ego Earth prescribed -
Until the day work felt like play
And the Sharing was what Shined.

1

It wasn't showing off your Star Light
For Galactic Pageantry-
It was the showing of Compassion
That shone the Brightest gleam.

So....

A Funny Thing Happened on the way to the Stage
That surprised her Sense of Purpose.
Could it be there's More than the 'part' adored-
It was much deeper than the surface:

The Journey to Oz Her Life was on...
The Journey to Higher Realms-
What good pursuit unless what you do
Can enrich the Lives you've felt?

For a Star can only Brighten Its Light
When Shared upon Its Path...
A Star Alone burns out its Glow
When it sees Life as One Task.

It's All a part of The Journey
To the Emerald City to Be.
And you discover your Path to get there,
Is more than just a 'Me.'

We are More than even our Dreams,
Much More than just ourselves.
Our POWER comes from Connection
With our Higher Source at Helm.

True Artistry in the Universe
Is More than meets the eye.
It often is accompanied by
Soul Mates who boost its Shine.

So when limited visions of Human Grandeur
Tempt your ego fly
Remember the Only Thing That Lives On
Is Who motivates the 'I.'

2020 Vision Check:

How Clear is what you See?
It interprets what you read.
The Lens you Choose,
Could Win or Lose
Your Inborn Destiny....

Choose to See
Through Eyes that find
Compassion where once fought.
And the world you See
Will Change and Be
A Kinder place than thought.

Let your Inner Vision See
Past all surface fears-
And soon your Vision Brings Revision,
Comfort to one's tears.
How Clear Is What You See?
Clarity Brings Peace.

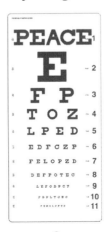

"A Holy Life"

It Is A Holy Life
Beyond All Human Reasons
With all its qualms and disagreements
It's Still A Path of Seasons.

Seasons of a Life Beginning
Seasons of it Ending
And In Between
Life Lessons Beam
Of Spiritual Transcending…

Help us Forgive our Human Hurts-
See Truth in each Transgression.
And Rise Above with Grace and Love
Make Us Your Revision.

It Is A Holy Life
Do Not Miss Each New Inning
What We Do Now
And Think - Is How
We Make Our Last Act Winning!!

A Little Shaky "Shakespeare"

For Today

(Aka: Some 'Shakes for Peers':)

"To Delete Or Not Delete, That Is The Question"

It's never the bite that kills you-
It's the venom in your veins.
It's never the words from someone rude,
It's your letting them remain.

There is Power in 'Delete'-
More than a button made...
The Power comes when it completes
Its mission to Upgrade...

Upgrade Up To Your Place Of Peace-
Forgiveness sets you Free
From all discomfort Judgment sees.
When Wisdom Doubts- Delete.

Let Grace Replace.......Let Be.

"Change The Way You Look At Things-
And The Things You Look At Change"
                                    -- Dr. Wayne Dyer

"Change the Way..."

A little baby butterfly,
Not seeing her Real Truth,
Struggled as her Wings would try
To fly from her cocoon.

The Change coming upon her
Was Too Close to know the 'Why'
Behind her inner angst unsure
Preparing her to Fly....

Then one day, her Breath Let Go
And she dared To Open Eyes
And Look at this Change
A different way-
And then to her Surprise...

She stopped rushing God's Process,
When an Opening Appeared
All on Its Own- without a phone
Without a call of fear...

She noticed The Most Beautiful Wings
Giving Birth before her eyes
She never would see happening
If she chose to see demise

Then as if by Magic what seemed Tragic
Appeared as New Faith Gained-
When She Changed The Way She Looked At Things,
The Things She Looked At Changed!

"Everyday Enlightenment"

It's The 'Everyday'
Enlightened Times
That makes a Holy Life -
Not just when 'Revelations' Shine
Upon a Special Sight.

It's the 'Little Moments' in between-
The Breathing In and Out
Reminding us that Light is Seen
When we're Aware Of 'Now.'

Now- This Moment- Look Around You...
God's Angels Sending Signs:
In The Smallest Things Are Truth-
Just waiting You To Find....

See the Flutter Of Butterflies
Flying by your Heart-
See the Shutter Of Wings That Fly
On the Highest Bird- What Art!

But Most Of All:
See The Miracle
God Made in The Form Of You-
Another Day Of Spending Life
On Earth In Love and Truth.

"The Who and Where Of You"

Why wait for Heaven?
Why wait for Peace?
Why wait for 'Better Times'?
If 'Heaven Is Within You'-
There's no 'New Place' to find.

Clear Away the Outside Views
That know not What Is Truth.
And Remember Who You Are Inside:
God's Power Lives In You.

Dare To Be The Change You Crave-
Dare Destiny Pursue...
God's Hands and Feet Are What He Gave-
Each Breath Is Love Renewed.

His Love Was Born As You.
Live LOVE and Live The Truth.

"Senior Moments"

I need to leave!
I forgot my keys
I found my keys

I forgot to leave.

The End

A Prince Story

"World Views From The Zoo"

The Giraffe and the Turtle
Became friends in the Zoo
Though they each had a hurdle
They had to jump through…

They looked at Life Through Two Different Views
Because of their own limits.
One could look Above the Two
And the other needed tickets!

The Giraffe looked Higher So Got Inspired
By a passing Flying Bird-
The Turtle saw nothing that transpired
But a feather drop unheard.

Their Points of View formed their Truth
From How they each were raised:
One saw Higher, One saw smaller
No Fault- just how they were made.

Then one day came pouring rain
And the Giraffe seeked lower shelter
And under a tree, the Turtle with glee
Peeked his head out of his cellar.

And Together they realized what a Blessing
This Pouring Rain became
For it Opened Up their hidden dressings
To meet with out a blame.

They met on Common Ground without
The limits of different views
And realized they're on a common route
To protect from this monsoon!

So when the rains pour on the Sane
And Humans judge their Truth
Remember we're All on the same plane-
Just different Animals in the Zoo!

"This Little Light Of Mine"

From the Firefly to Star Light-
To the Sun Light To the Moon.
There Is no Human Stoplight
On your Path Born to Pursue.

Let No One dim the Beams
God put Inside Of You.
Each has Their Own Purpose-
Each Leads to Your Real Truth.

So Shine On in the Light Of
The kind of Life That You Enjoy.
For God Breathed His Life Into
Your Expression- His Employ.

Your Real Job?

What Brings You Joy!

"The Millionaire & The Minion"

'Twas The Simplest of The Simplest Days,
The Simplest of all times-
When a little boy sat on a curb
With his Cornbread Tasting Fine.

As he dreamed of living Higher-
Dreamed of Higher Things,
An expensive shiny limousine
Drove past to see this scene...

An older feeble well dressed man,
Out his window looked
Longingly at the little boy
Until his cornbread shook.

"Sir," the boy then shyly said,
"If you're hungry, would you like This?"
To which the old man shook his head
And said he had One Wish:

"If only I could sit on a curb
And Dream and Eat Cornbread,
I would trade all riches that I've earned
Before Stress Makes Me Dead.

But no amount of money
Can give me back my Health.
If I could trade your milk and honey,
I'd give you All my wealth!

I'd trade you for a sunlit day
I could sit upon a curb,
And listen to the children play,
Listen to each bird.

But I can't hear a thing but ringing-
Registers in my ears-
The Joy I thought, Success I've caught,
Would calm my earthly fears.

For what you have is Priceless:
Peace of Mind to Dream...
There is no Price to Peace and Time-
It can't be bought, just seen."

As the limousine drove off, he waved
And left a Gift ne'er keener:
That Cornbread Is The Best Homemade-
And Your Own Grass Never Greener!

"The Power Company"

Who has your Power today?
Is it a circumstance gone wrong?
Is it a Dream in the hands of others
Where your control you found was gone?

Is it the view of those you once knew,
Now living who you thought you were?
Or one's unqualified opinion
Keeping you unheard?

What e'er the source of your remorse,
It's time to Take It Back-
As you see the world in front of you,
Go on the attack.

You forgot It's You Who gives 'Them' Power,
Every time your Insides shrink...
Into invisibility
That only you can see.

There's no attack- God has your back,
When your Heart's in The Right Place-
Of Pure Intention And Pure Ascension
Above this Worldly Place.

Who has Your Power Today?
The Decision's up to You.
Only You Control Your Insides,
And There lies what is True.

Lay not your Treasures in a transient world
Where Fame Fades Like The Sun.
Each New Day, New Life's Begun
Re-Born Within The One.

Take Heart, You're Never Done.
What's REAL?
The Power of Love.

"Hearing Aids"

Listen-
We'll Write Through You...
We'll use your fingertips
To type what type of Lesson Learned
You need for All That Is.

Listen-
We'll Live In You
To soothe hurt feelings deep
Our Wings will wrap around Your Truth
With Comfort your Soul Needs.

Listen-
We'll Confirm You
In Wisdom's Cloak Of Brave
So when others call when e'er they fall,
They'll not forget Our Name:
I AM ....
Shows You The Way.
What Will You 'Hear' Today?
Ask Angels when you Pray.

"The Currency of Kindness"

What Really Matters in the end
Is more than what we think
More than actions we defend
All over in a blink.

What Really Matters is how we spent
The Currency of Kind
Kindness to each Soul God sent
In our way too short lifetimes.

What's remembered: How We Felt
From others words and deeds...
Were their Intentions from The Well
Of Kindness in our pleas?

For Behind the Reads of Human Pleads
For Justice: Rights and Wrongs -
Is an underlying deep Soul Need
For Kindness to Belong.

It's not easy Being Human,
Every Soul has hurts to bear-
Tempered by each new one
Wondering Who may care.

So today when you meet Any One
On the street you find
What Matters in the long run:
Did you Remember to be Kind?

"In His Gentle Presence"

Be Gentle with each passing Soul
That comes across your Path...
Their Very Presence could Be The Essence
Of your Higher Purpose Cast.

Each Face you see is a Reflection-
In the Pool of Life so Deep.
Cast Upon your Soul's Direction
There's More To What You See...

Be Gentle with Each Passing Feeling
That comes across your Heart-
They have The Power to Guide your Seeing
The Truth of Who You Are.

Surrender To The Star

"Where Are They?"

In the Deepest Silence
Breathe In and Listen In
Inside You'll find The Science
Of Where Your Loved Ones Went...

Closer than your Heart beat
Deeper than your veins
They run right through you to defeat
What seemed to cause you pain.

In the Deepest Silence
Listen Deep Within
Let the The Unheard Depths of You
Whisper words unsent...

Angels Waiting
Upon Your Saying
"I'm Ready, Please Come In"
And Closer than the Breath you're Breathing,
New Destiny Begins...

..."But Not Too Long"

You can Rest -- but not too long.

You can Work -- but not too long.

You can Play -- but not too long.

You can Love -- but Never Long Enough...

That's Why There's Heaven.

"Word Baths"

Dear God, Please take the words escaped
Out of my mouth through critical gates-
And run them through your Filter Above-
Transforming them into Forgiving Love.

Cleanse and Purify each Thought
So that when they roll out
Only Goodness is caught.

Cleanse my Soul from North to South
Please Bless The Words That Come Out Of My Mouth!

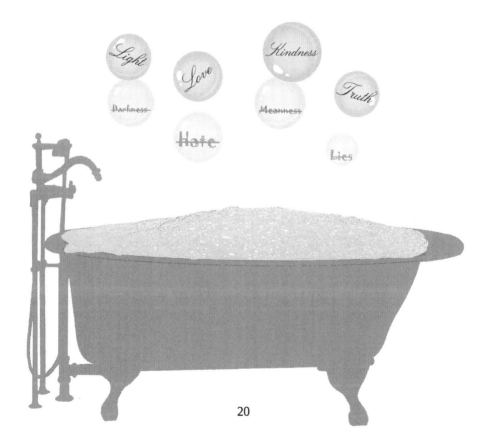

"To The Caring Ones"

This is for The Caring Ones
The Compassionate, The Daring Ones
Who Dare To Reach Out Of Themselves
To Help the hurt, To Heal, Make Well.

The Nurse, The Doctor, Caregiver, Responder.
Who Every Day Help those fallen under.
Who See the not so pretty in Life
And Bring Relief for the suffering strife.

Please Know We Are Grateful Beyond Human Words-
For Beyond Human Effort you came to this world.
You work with The Angels on a Mission Above.
You Light our Life's Candle-

You Shine Brightly God's Love!

"APolitical Asylum"
For The Lions and The Lambs

"What does Peace of Mind feel like?"
Said the Lion to the Lamb.
"I never stopped my Roar for Right
To try to understand."

The Little Lamb would run each time
She heard him creeping by,
But this time sensed a different sigh
From his normal beastly cry.

She knew not what to say to him,
Since different ways they speak-
So instead she let her Spirit send
What others thought was weak...

It was not a roar to prove her more
Or a Better One than he-
Instead she sent her Heart, her Core
Her Energy Unseen.

She simply laid there in her Peace
As Still as Still could be
Till he felt unthreatened, instead he reckoned
This a Peaceful Place to Be!

For around her for the first time felt
Defenseless and Calm
No need to pounce or views renounce
What reason now for all?

So curious, he crept beside her
So curious, in awe
And instead of scratch at where he's at,
He gently showed his paw-

And in that moment Little Lamb
Understood why he would scream
Each time she squeaked and ran from him
In fear he would defeat.

He was in pain from wounds unnamed,
Bruised from battles fought
But when her Defenseless Manner flattered
Relief was what she brought.

She gently bowed her head and said
In Silent Loving Prayer:
"Dear God Please Bless my Lion Friend...
Release our fears and cares."

"What does Peace of Mind feel like?"
Said the Lion to the Lamb.
"I never stopped my Roar for Right
To try to understand."

Then a silent wave of Peace he felt,
Without a word she answered.
His questions that no words could tell-
Unspoken words heal faster.

So there they stayed and learned to pray
By saying "Peace I Am"
And that began the Plan for Man:
When The Lion Lays Down With The Lamb.

"Sinventory"

-Each Night Before You Go To Sleep
-Each Morning When You Wake
-Each Moment You Spend In Between-
Soul Inventory Take:

Is there dis-ease within your Heart
O'er Something someone said?
Were You Kind or were you Hard?
Were You Soul or Ego led?

Do you carry blame inside?
Do you carry hurt?
Either One can be a lie
When Mis-Perception blurs...

How we 'See' holds The Key
How we choose To Be.
Let not your Inner Power bleed
Let not your Soul deplete.

Each time we let another's pain
Take our Power away-
They take away our Path To Sane
Our Path to Peace we Pray.

So next time your Heart feels justified
In being hurt by others,
Remember All comes from Inside:
We Reflect Each Other's Cover.

Compassion Heals Each Other.

"Comfort in The Uncomfortable"

Before a plane lifts from the ground,
Its engine must ignite.
Before a bird's new wings are found,
It has to prepare for Flight.

Every Stretch from Comfort Zone,
Is a Stretch in Consciousness
To rise into a new Unknown-
Takes Some 'Outrageousness.'

So why take all the trouble and risk?
Why not Stay Put in Peace?
Cause True Peace comes where True Life Is:
Creating's How God Sees.

True Happiness Is Ease-
When We Become What We're Born To Be.

For The 'Forgotten' Ones:

"The Distant Gardener"

A Flower never saw 'The Gardener'
Who ran the Land she bloomed...
She often felt she didn't matter,
If not noticed in Their Room.

Though she felt left out in their 'Big Leagues'
Of planting on The Hill,
She did her Best to pass the test
Of Living what was Real.

And then one day she Did feel noticed
By the Smallest One passed by.
The Glow upon their Smiling Face
Renewed her Purpose Prime.

And then she Got a Higher Meaning
Living In the Ego World -
That though she never saw 'The Gardener,'
Something Greater still occurred.

She saw that Life is So Much More
Than Positions known on High.
That Real Life is The Every Day
Each Soul that passes by.

For the Greatest One you're Put here for
Transcends Who earth has Seen-
"As ye have done it unto one of the least of these my brethren,
ye have done it unto me."

Take Heart -- God Always Sees.

"The Power of Being Gentle"

The room was filled with bigger folks
Powerful and Grand
Talking over each other
Each had to take their stand.

But as loud and domineering
Their Beings seemed to be
They all stopped their jeering
At the sight of One Baby.

Its gentle coos, its heavenly gaze
Its pure and innocent face
Made Bravado change its ways
When looked into the Eyes of Grace.

In every species known to man
Whatever their stance may be,
Will soften when they take the hand
Of an innocent small baby.

So whenever you feel you have no power
Think of how The Angels kindle --
The smallest flames that grow and tower
Through The Power of Being Gentle.

Identity Crisis:

"The Butterfly & The Bee"

A charming baby Butterfly,
Fresh out of its cocoon,
Flew right by a flower's side
That a Bee had stopped to swoon.

"What do You do?"
Whispered she, to not disturb its plight,
"Well, I'm here To Be The Bee I Be...
Making Honey's on my Mind!"

"O My, she sighed, wish that were I !
All I can do is Fly!
It's not in me to make Honey-
Just Smiles as I Fly By...."

Then the Bee looked longingly
At her Wings Of Wonder,
And softly chimed,
"Wish You Were I -
To Freely Fly through Thunder!"

Then an Angel from Above
Happened to hear their cries,
And shared some Wisdom Blessed in Love
For Dreamers who Reach High:

"If you only knew Who You Really Are,
You'd Never want to change
Into Another's 'Lucky Star'
When given Your Own Range...

If your shape was like a Bee's,
Then what Freedom you would miss-
To Fly so Freely with Wings appealing
To give a Butterfly Kiss!

And sweet Bee, your Buzz of Love
Would be quite 'Honeyless'
No more 'Honey Makin' Bub-
What Flowers you would miss!"

We're All Expressions of God's Glory-
Each a Unique Design-
And when we try to change our Story,
Our Author we can't find.

So Stay True To You
And God Will Too,
For He Made You For A Reason.
Fret Not, Want Not Another's 'Who'
Let Nature Be Its Season...

Then when you Breathe from The Depths of Peace
In Sweet Serenity-
Your Wings Will Fly, no need to Try-
FEEL Authenticity:

Your True Identity!

ONCE UPON A CHERUB TRIBE ...

"A Cherub's Last Gift"

For a Special Mission, of Angel's Kind,
Two Cherubs looked to Earth -
To Dance within a Special Time,
To bring their Parents Mirth -

They brought Joy & Love & Laughter
And Anticipation deep -
That spread to the Hereafter ...
Where God could Hear them speak -

Though their time on Earth was Brief,
At best, we're surely 'rented' -
To share a Space - in His Sweet Grace
... Then back - where we're invented.

Some stays are short - and some are long-
Measured not by Time ...
For in God's Real Eternal World,
Life has no 'End' we find ...

Just Journeys we are Given -
As Gifts to Special Souls -
That Share the Light they're livin'
In this Mom and Dad they chose.

Their Gifts of Celebration
Remain to Honor Them -
Reminding us to put out Trust
In a Higher Plan that lends ...

Little Cherubs to the Earth -
Their Dance lent from Above -
To learn from Little Angels' Wings
Their Lasting Gifts of Love!

31

"Once Upon a Baby's Cry ..."

There lived a Cherub Tribe-
Of Little Children Angel Souls,
That people thought had died.

They're Known upon the Higher Realm
As the Lights and joys of Heaven-
Reminding all Who enter There
Of All the Joy They've Given ...

They're also Known to Fly to earth ...
And show up in a Giggle-
They're the Light of Love at Christmas Time,
They're the Thought that makes worms Wiggle!

In fact, They're Flying By right now -
Though you THINK you cannot see them ...
Like the Air you Breathe - They're Very There -
Exhaling Love in Rhythm.

They're making Themselves Known today
In the Angels seen in stores ...
And Giggle to Themselves the shelves
That humans now adorn ...

In Truth they're More than Wings and Things
Of Earthly Human Form -
They live in the Land where Lovers Sing,
Within Love's Sweetest Core.

Would you really like to see them?
Have you wondered if They're there?
I'll give a hint - your time well spent -
Relax, I'll take you there ...

Just close your eyes and listen ...
Softly now - Think Peace -
Think how the Sunlight Glistens
On a snowy mountain's feet ...

Smell the cool and warmth at once -
As the Sunlight hits the snow -
As Loving Hearts can warm these parts
Of Life that hit us so.

Their Footprints left upon your Heart
Will Guide you throughout time ...
You only need to ask Them,
And Their Inner Light will Shine ...

And Open New Horizons
And Lighten up your Way ...
They bring Power to the Art of Fun -
Therein - the Power of Play!

We forget Earth is God's Playground,
As we learn through human games,
And Cherubs' "Jobs" are Earthbound
To Help Heal Human Pains.

As the Warmth of Sunlight melts the snow
On the Highest Mountain Peak -
So the Love of Baby Cherubs Glow
Upon 'grown-up' Souls so weak.

As we must become a Child again,
To Enter Heaven's Gate ...
The Good News is - There is no 'When' -
We need not have to wait!

There is an 'Outlet' Place when lost -
To Help us through these times,
When e'er you stop and 'Angel Shop'
Upon a Cherub's Tribe!

"Where Does a Cherub Feel at Home ..."

In the Land of 'Human Kind'?
The comings, goings - fast and slow -
Known as the 'Human Grind' ...

Where Does a Cherub choose to Land
To feel secure and safe?
Where language flows like sand through hands -
Where words don't have to wait ...

In the Land of Humans great and small
Who cluster in Group-a-likes,
Related folks who feel they're close -
By blood of 'Positive' types.

Within these clusters great and small.
Stray Cherubs often visit -
Disguised Outsiders are frequent riders
Upon their Wings exquisite.

To learn their Home lies not in Blood,
Relation, or outside Likeness --
But in the Inner Parts of us -
Where lives no wrong or rightness.

Cherubs learn as well as Humans -
To stretch their Wings' Perception ...
Beyond their Heaven's Peacefulness -
To Humanly Reflections.

For we all are Born of One Great Source -
If we just Relax. Enjoy It -
Breathe In and Let It Take Its Course ...
Herein Let God Employ It!

And recognize there is no place -
No Earthly Human Dwelling
Where Earthly Angels aren't at Home -
And constantly re-telling ...

Their Playfulness and Joyfulness
Expressed in Human Form -
Their Loving Universalness
Each Time a Cherub's Born...

Into the Hearts of Each of Us
In the simple every day ...
Where Does A Cherub Feel at Home?
In the Heart that Loves To Play!

"Cherub Chance-a-lot"

Where Tender Hearts and Souls would play
Within the pink and purple shades
Of Heavenly Eves and Earthly Days,
A Cherub 'Chanced' the earth -

Cherub 'Chance-a-lot' his name,
Known by the Tribe for mischief games,
Always playing hide & seek
With Happy Thoughts that Children seek ...

For Cherubs have the Gift and Power
To Turn a Soul's most pensive hour
Into Events that make one Laugh -
And once put 'OOPS!' in Epitaphs!

For Cherubs Born of God's Pure Thought
Come from Pure Joy - and never caught
Up in a world of hurt and sorrow,
For just Sweet Peace is All They Follow ...

So, our Little Cherub Chance-a-lot
Went on a Mission here to swallow -
All the sorrow He could muster,
And turn it into Holy Luster.

First He went to nursing homes
And put Funny Thoughts in Souls alone,
Then up to Children's wards He Flew ...
And put a Bird in Window's View -

Little Gifts he 'Chanced' around,
Without a word - without a sound,
Anonymous the Thoughts He Gave -
To Heal the feelings sorrow made.

If only for a Moment Last -
There still was Hope - the Die was Cast!
Like Seeds are planted for Flowers' Growth -
So the Smallest Thought of Sweetness Flows ...
Into a Heart where hurt is Known.

Then, on His Missions far and wide-
He heard a tender, little cry -
Of a girl 'grown-up' outside,
But in her heart, a child denied.

No one seemed to Know her Soul,
A homesick Angel with fallen goals.
Forgot She did- of Why She came ...
Caught up She was in Dreams of Fame.

Then 'Chance' brought her a second Thought -
Of the World Her Heart had fought:
The Thought came in a subtle suit -
Clothed in Peaceful, Loving Views ...

That made Her stop - and take deep stock
Into What She Felt - and What She Sought.
And then the struggle to exist
Amongst the world She would resist,

Took on a Calmer, Firmer Ground -
When She stopped and Heard for Inner Sounds:
The Sounds of Peace and Love She craved,
Lived INSIDE - not in the grave!

She planted all Her Childhood Dreams
She Thought were dead and tired unseen.
She took a 'Chance' to LIVE Each Thought
Of Purest Love and Peace She Sought ...

Not waiting for an 'outside sign' -
But relying on Her Holy Find ...
Of Inner Peace that Lives so Deep -
Amidst appearance of pain we see ...

She Dared to LIVE Her Purest Soul -
No matter what the outside told.
And just when she took a Breath from There,
'Twas Chance-a-lot This Moment Shared ...

And Earned His Place to Be Transformed
Into the Brightest Wings He's Worn!
For as He 'Chanced' His Love to Fly -
Another Caught His Higher Ride ...

Up to the Place where Night meets Day:
Into God's World - Where Cherubs Play!

"Taking Care of the Caring"

This is for those Taking Care
Taking Care of Life you share
Nursing those for whom you bleed
Who live in Faith, fulfilling need.

When Illness strikes the One you Love
It strikes you too- you cannot run.
You feel their pain, their victories gained
But still takes All to keep you sane.

But the irony of this Destiny
Is there's more to all than we can see
One represents the Whole of All
We're all connected, So must stand Tall.

And face adversities with Strength
For there's more at stake than we Think
We're all reflections of each other
What happens to one- affects the other.

So For All of those Taking Care
Please Take a Moment, and Breathe and Share
And Open Your Heart So Big you'll cry
For There You'll Find Your Angels Fly!

"What Is A Miracle?"

Is it an Answer to our Prayers?
Is it Help that comes from Hearts So Full
Is It Relief from all our Cares?

Perhaps The Greatest Miracle
Is far More than we Think-
Perhaps The Greatest Miracle
Comes when Life is on the Brink.

It's More than 'Diagnosis'
The kind that makes you sink-
It's More than Life's Prognosis
That it's gone within a wink.

I've lived a life that's Prayed For
Asking God for All.
And Prayed Again as ne'er before
When still bruised from all its falls.

And then the Miracle Appeared
Surprising all I feared.
It wasn't 'Outer Happenings'
Dependent on less tears.

It wasn't Just an Answered Prayer
For things To Be as we had wished.
The Miracle was So Much More
Than a Bucket List.

The Miracle we were Promised
Is a Given By Our Side.
That No Matter what, God's not finished
His Grace Will Still Abide...

Through Storms and Human Illness
Through disappointing times,
The Miracle is Forever Wellness -
The Eternal Kind Inside.

But you cannot claim this Holy Gift
When judging 'good' or 'bad'-
Or you will be blind to Hope you find
In His Joy amidst the sad.

So What Really Is a Miracle?
In uncertain Human Land?

It's The Heart that LOVES When times get tough-

That's the Miracle in Man.

"When You're Missing"

Why Do we cry for Loved Ones
And Those who have 'Moved On'?
Perhaps it's More than feeling Torn
And Missing Memories fond.

It's More than Memories in our Lives
Of happy times and sad-
For We're All a part of a Greater Art:
An Experience Called 'Man.'

We're all little pieces and fragments of God's
Expression while we're still here-
So when one leaves, each soul grieves
Missing a Piece of God so Near.

When This is remembered, all conflicts cease-
All judgments of hurts and wrongs.
We mourn - not scorn
We yearn- forlorn
For God's Love in Flesh Adored.

So Take Heed with Loved Ones Still on Earth!
Forgive- Give For your Soul.
For Beyond the 'Human' - there is no ruin-
As a 'Piece of God' Unfolds...

Living On -- Inside Our Souls!

The following Poem was written as a Special Request from a friend who was asked to explain to a young skeptic the Existence of God. Whew! A Tall Omnipotent Order for this Short Humble Human!

In Essence there Is no 'explaining' the All Encompassing Unexplainable -- especially in These erratic Times. Yet, with an Inspired, though limited, Mind and a pondering, though Open Heart, my Angels in the Wee Hours, brought to me the following Rhyme of Rhetorical Reason.

Here's Hoping my poetic attempt (inadequate at Best and Sincerely Heartfelt at worst) may help in some miraculous way. So Now, with the above 'Spiritual Disclaimer,' I give to you:

"The Good, The Bad and The Holy"

Where IS "HE?"
This talked about 'God'?
Where can we SEE
This 'Invisible' Odd?

So asked the Seeker
Disheartened Today,
When the world seems Weaker
With its Lost 'Evil' ways....

Is The Wind Really Real
When you can't see it near?
Can you explain how It Feels
When It sweeps past you here?

Its Results you Can see
When a leaf leaves a tree-
Swept Up by the seize
Of an Invisible Breeze....

43

How does the Design
Of This Universe appear?
Sunset to Sunrise
With Bird Songs in our ears...

How do our Hearts
Beat All on Their Own,
With The Breath we impart
Till the day we are gone?

Like Clockwork our World
Continues Its Course...
Until Man unfurls
And heads for Divorce-

The Moment we disconnect from this Life Force-
Is The Moment we lose our Direction from Source.

What 'Source' you may ask,
How do we know It Is Here?
Will Electricity last
When its Plug is not near?

We Are All Energy-
As Science has proved.
Yet Still It Is We,
The Unconscious, Unmoved.

Unaware if we Unplug
From This 'God' Who's our Source,
We unplug from This Life
And disengage from our Course.

The Existence of God
Is The Existence of Life-
Which takes Many Forms
Many Intricate Plights:

How else to explain the Perfection of Birth?
How each Living Morsel
Carries with it His Worth?

Does Higher Intelligence
Ask Belief It Is True?
Whatever Belief in Its Relevance,
Stars Still Shine Upon You...

Though our mere Human Minds
Cannot Grasp Magnitude,
We can Open Wide
Our Perception of Truth.

Pure Love Unconditional
Is the Yearn of each Soul,
Because the Irrational
Still haunts Human Goals.

Yet this 'Energy' begins
And ends The Same Breath-
As The Universe blends
Every Birth - Every Death...

Into New Life
As Expressions of 'Him'
Does 'He' Really Exist?
Ask each Breath that you Live.

We're All Expressions,
Evolving Impressions...
We Always Get Back What We Give.
An Acceptance of Love
Is Acceptance of Him.
Good or Bad, Pure LOVE
Is The GOD Who Transcends.

Which brings us back
To Reveal what you ask:
Does God Really Exist?
A Wondrous Thought Task!

I leave you to Look into The Eyes of a Child:
A Newborn from Heaven,
Unjaded by miles.

I Leave you to Innocence-
Both Inside and Above
Where there is No Defense
What God Is Made Of:

It Is All IT IS:

Unconditional LOVE.

"Blessings in Disguises"

So you've Prayed, Released and Let It Go....
But - What comes back Surprises-
Don't question God's Unseen Control:
There are Blessings In Disguises!

What Appeared could mean your Fall-
Angels There to Catch You!
What Appeared betrayed your call-
God's Plan Transcends What They Do....

For no man, no Power, no 'friend' who cowers
Can hold back your Destined Flight.
Just Keep Your Eye on Higher Power-
And Let God Turn Wrongs To Right.

Your Blessing's In Your Sight!
Blessings: Disguised Light!

"A Fractured Veggie Tale"

A Red Rose Once Was Planted
In dirt with Yellow Corn
Expecting to be granted
Equal treatment every morn.

They tried to call her 'Veggie'
They tried to keep her small
But Something she kept sensing
Was not right with All.

They watered her like all the others
And expected her to grow
Just like her 'Veggie Brothers'-
But a Surprise Was Soon To Show...

You can plant & tend & nourish-
But nothing can replace
The Original Nature flourished-
What Your Made Of Makes Its Case.

So Time soon grew Red Petals-
Amongst the yellow corn
She couldn't hide or Settle-
For What she was First Born.

The moral of this Fable
Is Clear as Yellow and Red
Just Bloom with All You're Able
And Grow Where e'er You're Led..
No Matter the dirt you're fed,
Nature Takes Care of The Rest.

Sonrise

May Light be in your Center
When the not so Bright appears
May Fright of Life ne'er enter
Where uncertain roads be near.

I Pray for Light to bathe our Eyes
To see Beyond Each Brother
And Recognize God In Disguise
Just waiting to Discover ...

The Sacred In Each Other.

"The Soul Circle"

Today I ran into a Heart
Broken with such Grief-
She Lost Her Love, Saw Him depart
Too Soon to Heaven Leave....

Then right after, flew in my Path
A NewBorn Family shared...
A Brand New Generation Cast
With Joyful Love and Care.

The Extremes Of Joy and Sorrow
Hit us every day-
To remind that Each Tomorrow
Is an Unexpected Play.

Could Death be a New Beginning
Upon The Other Side?
Could Birth be a kind of Ending
From Heaven to New Life?

Both Tears of Joy and Sadness
Come from The Core Of Soul
That Deepen Eternal Gladness:
Connects What Makes Us Whole.

In This Circle Of Life: We Grow.

"The Throw Back"

Someone Else's Assessment Of You
Is Only True for Them.
It Truly has Nothing to Do With You-
Their Thought Is Not The End.

Don't let Their Energy Penetrate
Your Essence Deep Within.
For Who You Are Is More By Far
Than what Someone Else may lend.

Take Your Deepest Inner Breath
And Blow it Back to Them -
Breathe So Deep- They Must Retreat-
You have Nothing to Defend.

When Their Thought invades your own,
Let it Bounce Back - Let Go!
Keep What You KNOW Deep Close To Home-
Let No One Crush Your Soul!

Be Who You Are -- Be Whole.

"The Time Train"

This Train moves through so quickly
Down these Tracks of Life,
Before the next scene comes in view
The last one's out of sight.

Keeping Focus on This Moment
Takes Attention Never Ending-
For as soon as you view and comment,
It's time for New Beginnings.

The Highs and Lows and Hills and Valleys
All meld into One-
The One Consistent that always rallies
Is your Inner Lit God Son.

So when the Night Feels Much Too Long...
And you feel too stuck to move,
Remember This Train's Still Moving....
Next Stop :
Is Up To You.
Follow The Map Of Truth.
Become What You Pursue.
Regardless, Life Still Moves.

"The Trust Worthy Life"

Do you remind your body to Breathe
Each Moment of every day?
Do you remind your Heart to beat
When your own mind may stray?

Do you remind your Blood to flow,
Your hair and nails and ears to grow?
Your stomach to digest its food,
Your eyes to see ahead of you?

Then why not Trust The Rest to God-
Just as you do in your own bod?
Why not surrender each Dream So Tender
To The God With Plans for Every Gender?

The God Who Breathed His Breath In You
Also made Your Destined Route
So next time you're lost and Searching Truth:
Just Trust Who Gave This Life To You!

Your Path's Unique-
You're One, Not Two.

"The Turnaround"

If Something doesn't go the way
You trusted and been told-
Disappointment in their ways
Can hurt Peace In Your Soul.

Even if you're justified
In blaming the other-
It just comes back to hurt your side
And you carry their Energy further...

Do you wanta 'Be Right- or Happy?'
What Price Peace To You?
Forgiveness lets go the trappings
That keep you from Love's Truth.

Breathe Deep and Send Them PEACE To Heal-
Let Go what you can't control-
And You'll Become What you wished were Real:
You'll Become The Change and Grow!

"Life: The Ultimate Improv"

"The Holy Spirit will give you the words to say
at the moment when you need them." -- Luke 12:12

When people often ask me:
"How Do You Come Up With That?"
To be Honest, I Am Amazed Each Day-
Cause I'm Surprised by these 'Chats!'

Plan as I may 'Just What' I'll say
Is Changed by Circumstance.
Not One Moment Is The Same-
And I'm forced to take a Chance.

But God gives us
'In-Sure-ance' -
Inside we Can Be Sure:
The Channel's There,
Tune In with Care-
And His Words Will Come To Cure.
Surrender To Endure...
The Sweetest Words Speak Pure.

"The Ultimate Star Searching"

I've Dreamed of Stardom, I've dreamed of Fame,
For all the world to know my Name.
I've Dreamed of being so much In Love,
Through songs I'd sing, I'd feel Love's touch.

Then in my years of nature's prime
I feared my time was passing by ...
Still on the path of learning lines
And still not knowing what place I'd find.

And in my search for Spirit's Truth,
For Guidance concerning what next to do,
I found my Quest for being Best
Was answered in an "Inner" Quest.

My Faith was questioned in those tough times;
My only option, to give up "I"
And turn unsureness over to God
To be transformed by one mere thought ...

Of something Greater than earthly goals,
The Great Creator of all our Souls.
Then Focus changed from "What can I?"
To something better in "Who am I?"

My wait for 'Stardom' woke me Up
From stops and starts the world's made of.
Instead of waiting for "outer" breaks,
The Greatest One, Inside, I take.

Then the chance to sing to a little girl
Warmed my Heart like an oystered pearl,
And all these years of searching Love
Was found within, just as Above.

Now whatever Higher Spirit's planned
I've learned He'll lead me by His Hand ...
Whatever fame or stardom Be,
The Greatest Love lives Inside of Me!

"The Unexpected Signs"

When unexpected Obstacles
Appear in your 'Every Day'
Don't be alarmed or let them disarm
What you Know your Path To Play.

Before The Castle of Completion
Is reached to meet your Goal
Is when The Dragon in Ego's Fashion
Appears to test your Soul.

Keep Sight on The High-
Keep Up On The Try!
It's The Path Of The Yellow Brick Road...
The monkeys may fly and distract in the night-
But it's only a Sign You Are Close -

Your Journey to Oz unfolds often Odd
In ways unexpected- untold.
Hold Onto Love- Through it All - Always LOVE
And your Heavenly Path Will Unfold!

"Tuning IN"

Have you ever felt Sooo Tired.........
Even your Breathing's feeling Late?
Have you ever felt 'EXpired'
Before your Destined Date?

When Life gets Overwhelming-
To the point you need to Stop-
That's a Sign, Tune in Divine
To the Station called "I Got."

"I Got This!" Say your Angels-
Assigned to your Life's Work.
"I Got This!" Say "Untangle!"
Please Strengthen Inner Worth.

And to your Side will Rush Brigades
Of Help You Know Not Of.....
You are Their Job when times get tough-
To Bring Help from Up Above.

"Help!" Is a legitimate Prayer,
Hold Nothing Back Inside-
Tune Into God's "I Got This!"
And Watch Your Spirit Rise!

"Turning Tides"

When The Life You've known
Seems stripped away-
With disregard for Love,
Hold on to Promise of God's Better Way-
Keep Your Sights Above.

Never Lose Heart!
Never Lose Hope!
When what the world does
Are Blows to your Soul-

Your Ultimate Purpose
Untouched By The Throws-
Hold On and Hope On...
Your Future God Knows!

Your Protection Is Love
Your Direction Is Growth.

"U Talkin' To Me? U Talkin' To Me??"

Don't listen to that 'Voice!'
You know- That 'Voice' Inside Your Head!
That Discourages your every Choice
In The Path that you are Led.

ANYTHING That Sees The Worst
In Others- Or In You,
Could Never Come from God's Son
Could Never Come from Truth!

So Listen Not when you Are Fraught
With thoughts that bring you down.
Block it Out- Turn It Around -
And Let Your Soul Be Found!

Find Yourself and Ground Yourself
In The Glory God Pursues.
Base It On Where You Come From:
In LOVE You'll Find Your TRUTH!
Who's Talkin'?
Ain't always You.

"Up In the Trees"

Outside my window, the Tips of Trees-
Touching the Sky, So Still in the Breeze.
High Up Above the Chaos of City
Peace In the Trees,
In Nature, no pity.

In the Hustle of Human,
We forget to see Peace
In the Haste of Pursuin'
We Resist the Retreat...

Where Up in the Trees
Looking Up, we are Soothed
Seeing God's Peace-
Looking Up, We See Truth.

"Telling Time"

The Clock is ticking...
Each Breath - Till One
Be The Day It's Ending...
Too Short for Done.

Each Soul A Path
Each Life A Task
Respect Each Cast
Unknown To Last...

The Clock Is Ticking...
Don't Mute Its Sound
Each Tick Reminding
Life's Sacred Ground.

Eternal Breath
Breathe Life Profound!

"What Time Is It?"

What a Minute Means Is Relevant
To the State that you are in.
To some in Joy it's evident
It goes too fast to spend!

To some in pain it lasts all day
Begrudgingly Slow ...
To some in Love- It Stops Above
Into a Land Unknown.

Time is All Subjective
A Chart while we are here
Choose wisely your Reflective
Through Eyes of Love or Fear.

Before we reach The Timeless
Our Clocks no mercy show
Each Minute Here Is Priceless
And Determines Where We Go ......

Let Love Tell Time .... And Grow!

"The Compassion Fashion"

When your Heart is Hurt
By Misspoken Words-
And you yearn to return their Action,
Remember The Only Word that works-
Remember First:
Compassion.

When your Deed's Ignored
By those Adored-
And you miss a Kind Reaction,
Remember The Only Path To More...
The Feel That Heals:
Compassion.

For no matter where we each come from,
We Reflect All Human Fashion.
We're here to Learn to Heal Concern-
We're Here To Bring Compassion.

Let Compassion
Be Your Reaction.
Heal Deep
In The Cloak...
Compassion.

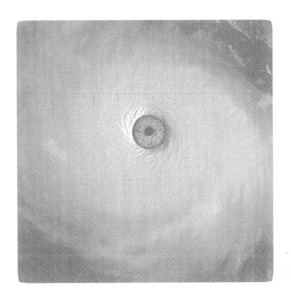

"The 'Eyes' Have It"

Why STILL in The Eye of a Hurricane?
Cause That's where Its Power IS.
As Chaos spins and Cries Begin,
Inside Its Calm Transcends.

The Power Of Life's Greatest Force
Comes from What's Inside-
Be Still in The Eye Of A Hurricane,
And Let Calmness Rule Your Ride.

The Powerful Inner Eye
Sees Through, Lets Peace Reside.

"What Then After Enlightenment?"

The Wise Old Sage was asked:
"In Holy Weeks we still must seek
Our Worldly 'Practical' tasks?" :(

Then The Kind Wise One looked Up -
And took the wood he carried...
And said "The only difference, Child,
Is the Smile when tasks must tarry."

The wood needs chopped-
Life never stops...
Tasks just change with time-
But Not The Reason Behind Each Season
Even with Life's weary signs.

What makes Each Week a Holy One-
And Each Day of Your Life,
Is not Events you can't prevent
Or the withstanding of your strife.

The Power of Enlightenment
Is The Joy that Lives Inside.
And with no Reason thru Each season
Still Shares a Heartfelt Smile.

An Inner Knowing that All That's Flowing
Is Temporary Flight-
Practice Flights both Day and Night
To earn your Wings of Might.

So Chop your wood and Carry water-
Search Joy in all your tasks.
And Remember when your Soul Feels bothered,
God Just Waits For Us To Ask...

"Cycling"

And the Sun Comes Up Again
In ritualistic blend
Shining upon the End
While other New Life Begins ...

The Cycle of Life is sobering
As Nothing stays the same
Except The One Thing Covering
Us all through Joy and Pain.

Invisible Wings envelop us
As we free fall through our lives
And The Son comes Up again
To meet us on The Other Side...

"When Destiny Detours"

Struggling With Circumstance?
Fly into The Winds Of Change —-
Even when Creativity
Others keep from Range.

Out of Range Of Rhyme and Reason,
No choice but to Carry On-
Out of Range Of Creative Season,
Keep Flying, Right or Wrong.

As the Fragile Wings of a Butterfly
Are praying to The Sky:
Out of the blue a cloud comes by-
With an Angel's soft reply:

"Little One, Flying into Sun,
Don't you know No Outside force
Can take away what God has made.
Remember Your Soul Source!

The Creative Keep Creating -
No matter Change of Course.
Go Within, Be Strong- Relating
To Your Creator's Inborn Force.

Times of Change know not your name.
They're Neutral- Circumstance.
The Magic is Surrender's Fame-
To Give a Second Chance."
Hold On-
Make Chance Your Dance!

"When Dreams Change"

Cast Not Your Dreams
Beyond Love's Reach-
For Some Can't See That High!
Bless Them and Move On To See
No one Can Take Your Smile.

Time to Let Go and Let God Heal
All That's Gone Before...

As said, 'Go High, when Low looks real'-

Let LOVE Lead Through New Doors!

"What Is 'Genius?'"

What Is 'Genius?'
Said The Thought to the Page,
What Is Kindness?
In a world of such rage...

Then The Thought turned around
Transforming Soul Sounds-
Releasing Its Dream
New Thoughts to rebound.

The Answer Appeared
As Mystically Clear
As The Rainbow
Comes After The Rain:

The Cycles of Life
Transform Wrongs into Right
Each Time Man Learns from his Pain....

Bringing to Life
Healed Joy After Strife-
Is The Genius
Of LOVE to The Sane.

"WHO ARE YOU?"

Are you your Name?
Your claim to Fame?
Are you a Definable Person?
Are you Who Others 'Think' You Are?
Or is your Dream still Nursin'?

Are you shot down under their Crown?
Do 'They' Define Your Star?
Take You Back!
Take You Back!
You Are NOT Who THEY Say You Are...

Of making others be so much less
Than They Think They Are Born To Be.
Be Oblivious to 'Outside Powers'
Who Think They control your 'Me.'

Keep Your Eye on What Is High-
Don't let them steal your 'Great.'
Don't Worry- It's ne'er too late
To BE Who Your Soul Dictates.

WHO ARE YOU?
Don't let others define you.
You Are Who Your Creator Creates.
Just BE...and Come Home To Great.

"Window Washing"

She looked Outside her Window
The Morning Light shown through
Yet from the Inside Looking Out-
Appeared more than morning dew.

Looking through the Window's grime,
Her perception soon Realized:
Her Need to Clean the surface-
And so she went Outside...

After streaks and cleaning squeaks,
Her View was Still askew
Until she Looked around and found
Another Thing To Do

Instead of Fixing Outside blocks-
She Cleaned the Inside Glass
And soon discovered her View was covered -
It was an 'Inside Task!'

Then as she Cleaned from the Inside Out,
The Outside Clearer came....
But not until she took care of First -
The Inside Window Pane.

So when you search Outside to see
What's Really Going On,
Make sure your Inner Lense is Clean
To See True Right from Wrong.

"Here's Looking *At You, Kid..."*

'Who' is looking out of your eyes...
And into the eyes of Another?
All species share that common Disguise-
Every Creature, Sister and Brother.

When you peer into a Baby's Eyes
Or a Kitten or a Rabbit,
Did you ever wonder 'Who's' looking back at You?
Could it be More that they Inhabit?

Coming from Star Stuff of Nature,
So many Creative Designs...
Living, Dancing and ever Romancing:
Expressions of The Divine-

In the Image of God, Love Shines!

"Words Most Powerful "

The Most Powerful Prayer
You can say Anywhere
Is more Simple than Simple can Be-
And Yet it Speaks Truth-
It Speaks Gratitude
Affirming The Good that you See.

The Most Powerful Prayer Catches All Unaware,
Cause what's Simple Speaks Peace to what's True.
It's The Best we can Share When a Heart Shows Its Care.

Love's Most Powerful Prayer Is:

"THANK YOU!"

"While Waiting In The Wading Pool"

TRUST where you are -
Where e'er you are-
It Matters Not Your Space.

God Has a Plan.
Ne'er Give Up - Just Stand.
And in Your Now Embrace...

You're Born To Live A Destiny-
No Matter WHAT You See...
Adorn your Soul with Higher Goals.
You'll Be What You're Meant To Be.

Only God Controls The Sea.
Hold On- And Trust His Lead.
The Shallow End runs Deep
When You Trust Your Maker's Keep.

Though the Road ahead on this Earth may feel uncertain -- Here's One thing Faith Will make Certain:

When Life Events don't happen as 'expected' and The Powers that Be have 'other plans,' Take Heart! At the other end of 'The Blizzard of Odd' is the Emerald City of Hope and Inspiration where Lessons of Faith are learned DEEP within you. Then you know you can survive Anything!

"The Blizzard Of Odd"
(While Awaiting 'The Thaw')

When the world has 'Frozen Moments' -
And we freeze inside our tracks,
Perhaps they're Frozen to watch our Breath-
As demands cry out: Relax!

When the world has stopped our goings-
And we're forced to Stop Pursuits-
Perhaps they're Frozen to Take a Breath-
And warm our walking shoes.

Our Comfort Zones are Challenged
When the 'every day' is thrown-
A Wake Up Call... Convenience Thaws
And reminds how no one owns....

How can we judge just 'Why' things happen-
The meaning runs too deep...
Beneath the snow and freezing cold
That Blooming Rose still sleeps...

So Take Heart Inside Your Heart!
Take Heart, what e'er Life brings...
Blessings wait, let Time partake.....
The Process Still Brings Spring!!

Hold On, Sweet Friends, Hope Sings!!

"Our Four Legged Angels"

When I see you in Heaven,
Will Your Soft Spirit Be
Bathed in Fur looking back at me?
Cause you brought Heaven down here to earth-
Please promise I'll hear your sigh and purr...

As our Hearts endured as you felt hurt
Sweet Angel Pet, My Child of Fur
I can't imagine more Angel's Worth-
As you earned your Wings at your Re-Birth.

This is Dedicated to Any Of You
who Deeply missed a "Homecoming:"

"Good Bye to Butterfly"
(When Unknown The Reason 'Why')

Feel in every warm embrace,
The Missing Of Another.
Their Loving Haunting ne'er Erased-
Just moved to move on further...

Up The Trail To Heaven's Door-
Each Journey like none other...
Though miss we do our "Me & You"-
Each Soul Remains Our Brother.

The Memories Of Each Purr & Prance
And Loving Look Of Home,
Will never leave Our Hearts-
You Are-
Our Soul That Never Roams.

For We're One-
We're All God's Own.
Inside, We Know You're Home.

"Whispy"
The Whispering Cat

This is the Story of a Magical Cat-
Not like a Garfield Or A Cat in the Hat.
This is the Story of an Angel Stray-
Whose name is "Whispy"-
"That's What Whispy Would Say!"

Showing a mysterious, friendly Soul,
Fluffing her tail to say "Hello!"
Since she couldn't talk in Cat Meows,
She 'Whispered' sweetly as she knew how.

Her former Peeps named her "Steve??"
On her Chip, we would read,
From far off states -Came Here To Be,
To fulfill her Kitty Destiny!

She had already been 'fixed'
Which we did not know-
Till the Vet saw her stitched,
Where she'd been re-sewn!

A Miracle Cat With Powers she showed
With family or feline-
Sweet Love from her Always flowed...
With animal or mankind...

Even the other lost strays came to play,
A Diplomat's Dream, With her kind gentle ways.
She fluffed up her tail -And walked with a strut,
As if to say: "Hey! Let's Play and Have Fun!"

Though Silent she was, when she tried to Meow,
With a faint little whisper, She'd purr with each prowl...
And sit on our lap, and with Love relay
Her own quiet rap:
"Here's What Whispy Would Say":

"As you enter a room,
Begin with a Stretch——-
Stretch out and then zoom
Your eyes on the rest...

Sit and Be Still
Wherever You Lay-
Each Moment Stay Real!
Is What Whispy Would Say...

Explore each new View
That is coming to you -
Be it a move
Or a taste to pursue...

For Each View IS New
It's More than it seems
Especially when viewed
On Kitty TV!

Each Day's an Adventure-
Kitty Zen is the way!
Let fear never censor-
That's What Whispy Would Say...

When the world is in Chaos
Around You, Be Still-
Curl Up and Be True,
Be Gentle, Be Real.

Love all your Humans,
As Only Human they are,
They know not the pursuin'
Of Peace As You Are...

So she continues her Mission
To Bring Peace to Our Days,
Until Humans will Listen
To What Whispy Would Say...

As we end with a 'Whispy' Meow To Our Prowl,
Our Whispy Says:
"Peace-
Sweet Peace To Your Now!"

(As paw printed by"Whispy,
The Whispering Cat")

"Chirp Of The Morn"

Chirpy has a 'Window Seat,'
Looking out at Life.
Watching every bird that tweets-
Every leaf the wind flies by.

She earned her name from 'Chirping' fame-
As she Chirps each cat's meow.
A Diva Cat, May Let you tame-
But to no cat will she bow.

She teaches us to Play & Crave
The Joy Of Being Alive!
No Great Goals- Each Moment Knows-
The Path to Paradise...

The mischief of the day awaits
As the Crack Of Dawn she Greets-
The mysteries that tempt our fate-
From a Front Row 'Window Seat.'

Next Flight?
Just Jump, You'll See!

"Luv, Hug & Grub"

Life At Its Best
For our Sweet Pets
Some Luv & A Hug
& Some Grub & Some Rest.

What to do when they have a day 'Off'?
How 'bout a nap and a fun little romp?

If we come back in some different form,
I'd vote to devote my next life to Be Born
Into the Arms Of some 4 Legged Love
Unconditional, Original
God's Gift from Above.

To only need Love, a Hug & Some Grub!

(Kitties passing through)

"The Land of Babies & Kittens"

Where do Kittens & Babies go
Inside their Deepest Sleep?
Where do their purrs & sighings Flow?
Where do they find such Peace?

Being closer to where they're from
In that Heavenly Realm So Sweet
It must be easier than some
Grown Human's stumbling feet.

Back Home Inside where Spirits roam
Back Home where lives Pure Peace
Back Home where Only Purest Love
Is recognized Complete.

The Land of Babies & Kittens
Have a lot that they could teach
Especially to us 'Grown Ups'
Who ne'er practice what we preach...

That it's More than words which mend our hurts:
It's Comfort, Warmth Within
The Purest Parts Within our Hearts
That Trust Where Life Begins!

"A Cat Nap for The Mindful"

Take us to where Kittens sleep
In their soft & furry trance...
All curled up in Total Peace
So far from raves & rants.

Take us where the Innocent-
The Babies Newborn Be.
Extend their time so shortly lent
Before the Worldly see.

Even Baby Predators
In Nature's Circle of Life-
When they sleep, can be so sweet
And forget were prone to fight.

This world could use a 'Cat Nap'-
A Time to curl & coo...
Then return with Calm they learned
With Peace To Carry Through.

"The Complacency Process"

A comfy place inside that shell
Peaceful, Quiet, Still.
"Gee, I could stay forever, Swell!"
So the oyster laid back to chill.

But as the days turned into nights
God had other plans
In her slumber, she forgot to remember
Just why she met The Sand.

"Wake Up, my friend!"
The Sand would rant
Wake Up, It's Time to plan
Your next step upon this ship
In the ocean of 'Yes, I Can!'

But the oyster got too comfortable
Settling where it's safe-
Not realizing in her retiring
Is short lived Peace to take.

Yes, for awhile it's comfy cozy,
But it's not how True Peace works.
One cannot really rest so rosy
Until you Focus First ...

On that Light peeking through your shell
Guiding your next Growth-
Tis the secret of Your Truth to tell
You're meant to live in Both.

Without the shell there is no Well.
Without The Sand, no Growth.
Together They work Hand in Hand
This Life depends on Both.

As the irritants of Life that rub us
So often the wrong way,
Are really polishing the dust that grabs us
That forces us to play.

A round of Russian Roulette in Life
Not knowing what will fire:
Should we pull the trigger Strife
Or put it down, retire?

But That Grain of Sand won't let us alone
And keeps knocking at our shell-
Dear God, will this Human Angst e'er go?
Or are we doomed to Human Hell?

And The Great Creator answers back
As His Wisdom does unfurl:
"My Child, don't take life as attack-
How else Become a Pearl?"

"Having Mercy"

When we say "God Have Mercy,"
I wonder what He'd say back...
Would He wonder "How Can 'He' Have Mercy?"
When His Mercy Has No Lack.

Could it Be, it should Be 'We'-
Having Mercy On Each Other?
Since God IS Mercy, He Already Has
Each sister and each brother.

It's We who should 'Have Mercy'
On Each and Every One.
It's We who live Uncertainties
Wishing 'Someone Else' would come.

While God Just Waits with Patient Arms
To come through Ours to Comfort...
He waits for Us to BE the Mercy-
To wake our selfish Slumber.
Have Mercy, All Who Suffer.

(While writing this poem, I had just 'spoken' with my Mother who had passed away 2 yrs. earlier that month. When I re-read what I wrote, in the last line of the first stanza I noticed I wrote the pronoun 'Hers' instead of 'His.' I could swear I was thinking I wrote 'His' :~)

"Heart Vibes"

When You Speak From Your Heart,
You Speak Who You Are.
So don't be concerned if others depart.

For whether or not you Speak what you mean,
It's Always your 'Energy' that others will Read-

It's Always your 'Vibes' -
Your Truth that precedes.
No one can hide behind words that we see...
-
For The 'Truth Who You Are'
Is The Star Of This Play.
Best to Be Real-
God Finds Out Anyway.

"Holy Homework"

Who's Your 'Divine Assignment'?
What would God have you do today?
It may come as Unknown Surprise-
No need to know 'The Way'...

It may be Someone sent to you
Who challenges your Faith-
It may be Something meant to do-
An unexpected Fate.

Whatever It Is, It's Meant For You:
To Be God's Hands and Feet.
Whoever resists The Good you Do-
Will not forget 'The Meet.'

We're All 'Seed Planters' In His Garden-
No One can force it grow.
We must not let the weeds dishearten
The Path The Pure Must Go.

For in due time, the Flower
Bends Its petals to The Light-
And Thanks Life's Unexpected Shower
For nourishing Its Sight.

Each Encounter: A Holy Rite.

"Re-Name The Mundane"

The Secret to Every Day Happiness
Is Simpler than you think-
Not necessarily a Dream Come True
Or a Super Spectacular Event.

Real Life is made of 'Practical Moments' -
Little Things that Have to be done ...
Dishes in the sink and company comin'
All over New Chores Begun.

If we could Find the FUN in All-
The Common Things we Do,
Wouldn't Life be More Than 'Waiting'
For that Dream you're Looking To?

Step by Step, our Joy Invests
Truly to Higher Goals...
But may we not forget
The Clock Still ticks
In the 'Meantimes' that Life Holds.

So Today, Take Some Time to Take some Fun
And Challenge Yourself to find
Unexpected Joy in Every Employ
The Mere Joy in Being Alive!

A Poet's Thank You Note

"It's Not Me -- It's You"
Said The Poet To The Sage,
Each Day I Pray in Gratitude
When Your Message Comes my way...

Angel Thoughts God Sends Through -
In So Many Special Ways.
It's Up to Us To Stay Tuned
To His Higher Truth Each Day.

And When We're 'In Tune'-
Spirit Knows What To Do:
Downloading Wise Files
Love's The Reason We Do!

"It's Not Me - It's The Message"
Just a 'Messenger' Am I-
So Grateful These Rhymes
Through These Fragile Times.

I Thank You Humbly and Deeply
Profoundly Joyful Completely-

As I Feel Your Wings Embrace my Soul.
Use my words as a Comfort
to your Children who've suffered-
I Pray to be Used for God's Goal.

"Living Your Vision"

It's Not Where You Are-
It's Who You Are...
We Each Have Special Missions.
Shine Your Light As The Brightest Star
Life is A Transition...
God Blesses Each Position-
Live Your Highest Vision.

When perceiving what is Truly Important in this world, I am reminded of the story of George Bailey in "It's A Wonderful Life." When you are rich with Loving Friends in whose life you make a Difference, Your True Spirit Shines upon the world around you. God uses Your Gifts as you play The Most Valuable Part No One Else Can Play: Being You!!

Shine On, My Gifted Versatile Friends: Shine On!!

"Stopped Watches"

It's That Hour in the middle of the night-
That Hour in the middle of Life:
Too late to make a mis-take right-
Too early for Sunrise....

It's That Hour in the middle of fright,
Not knowing where to turn-
When circumstance comes to dance
Upon more things to learn.

You know your Faith
You know God's Way
Is Trust in All Concerns,
Yet when That Hour comes to play,
Your Human Heart still yearns...

For All The Conflict in this world
To Finally go away,
For All that is that's So unsure
To dawn on Brighter Days.

No matter how much Peace
Your Own Faith Feels So Sure,
Still you can't forget The Rest-
What Others must endure...

Until the last Child goes to bed
Not hungry any more-
Until the last Soul understands
The Peace of Heaven's Door...

Until We Tune to Higher Sounds
That speak to Higher Grounds,
Total Peace cannot be found
In Human webs still wound.

So when That Hour in the middle of night
Tries to steal your Peace,
Hold onto fast your Inner Sight
And see how Angels See:

We're not just One, We're WE.

God, Throw Down Your Keys!

Forgiveness Unlocks Peace.

"Surfing In The InnerNet"

The Morning Broke
With nothing changed-
Or so it seemed the world...
Except when woke Up I to Pray
With a frightened little girl.

"I want to be Your Presence, God,
Without the pain of fear.
You're a BEING - Not a 'Doing' - Here-
You're Closer than what's Near."

But how can this frail little fish,
Who swims alone so deep,
Keep withstanding Waves not landing-
With fins instead of feet?

"I see above the Ocean's tide-
Then I'm swept beneath Its Power-
I drown with sounds Of clocks Inside-
Yet, lose sight of the Hours."

And as this little fish rides waves
To where she cannot see-
The vastness of the Ocean fades
Its Possibilities....

Then the Moment her Soul
Floated up-
To The Light upon the water...
Focusing while Looking Up
Above what currents fought her...

The Waters that surrounded her
Spread like windblown sand-
As if were being swept away
By some Higher Hand...

And in that fraction of a space,
God rescued her- The Truth:
"It matters not
Which 'Wave' you take-
For I AM The Ocean Too!"

"Angel Calls"

Calling On All Angels
With Protective Wings to spread
Your calming energy wrap around
All our Wounded Friends!

Our Hearts and Thoughts are With You
Our never ending prayers
Dear God please send your Miracles
Protect All Everywhere!

Who?

"The Great Define"

What Are You Defined By?
Who Do You Say You Are?
Are you Defined by the Checks you Sign?
Or the model of your car?

Or Your Age On Each Birthday:
Your Face, Your Eyes, Your Genes?
When in fact you're More Than That:
You're Every Age You've Seen.

Define a Leaf, and it will leave
When Winter comes to be.
Define a Seed and see it Freed
When Springtime makes a Tree.

We're Beyond Defining-
By Color, Brains or Bod-
For In the End, Each Life's Rewinding
Back To The Heart of God.

"The Greatness Choice"

The Chance Is There-
The Dream You Wear
In your Soul that Guides Your Feet...
To walk In Its Vibration Shared
With your Greatest Joy and Peace.

Don't let the energy of others
Sneak into your Highest Self.
Don't let reactions cause distractions
That shake your Spirit's Health.

Never Give Less - Give ALWAYS Your Best-
ALWAYS What you're Capable of-
Or you'll pay with the rest
Mediocrity's Test-
Of Feeling you're not Enough.

It will haunt you in quiet desperation -
When you Know Inside Something's Not Right.
Do not ignore these subtle sensations-
They're Signs to Get Back to The Light!

The Price Of Not Being
ALL You Can Be
Is too Much to owe your Soul.
The Plight Of Living In Integrity
Is The Path To Becoming Whole.

"The Grace Place"

Where do you take a past mistake
That Haunts you like a Chase?
Take it where True Peace is made:
Engage God's Place Of Grace.

What do you do when words won't come
To correct what Hurt your Fate?
Take it to The Master's Plate-
In God's Place Of Grace.

No Depth you've buried-
No Guilt you've carried-
Whatever You May Face-
Is Too Great for His LOVE to Replace:

Embrace God's Place Of Grace.

"The Open Mind"

Living in Awareness-
This short stay here on the earth,
Is Living in More Careness
Of the ways we search for worth.

Each Breath, Each Thought
Each Cause that's Fought is a Step towards Eternity...
Each deed, each plead for Justice Sought
Will Lead to Where we'll Be.

Living in Awareness-
Each Person that we meet
Is a symbol of God's Fairness:
We Sow the Seeds We Reap.

Our Choice Is How We See-
We Become The Soul We Seek.
Live In Truth- Be Free!

"When Business Lives As Business Does"

An Eye Opening conversation
With a person of position.
About the feelings of actions
Of those in her Transition:

"I have No 'Stress' in dealing
With others in their jobs-
I've learned to 'let it go' at home.
I live with out a sob."

Interesting, I thought to myself,
As I sensed no emotion there.
How fortunate the company
Who can justify 'no care.'

What's More Important in this Life?
Is it Letting Go Of All?
What place does Empathy employ?
Unyielding Rules The Call?

When that Final Clock is punched Above,
What's More Important Then?
The way you ruled with Corporate Glove,
Or the way you treated Friends?

"...In Exploration of Corporations"

Whatever happens in Corporate Thought
Of what's respected, and what is not,
Will come and go as years unfold -
But it's the Human memories that make life Gold.

One can try to take your Truth
But not the Talent that created you.
So push down the Spirit as far as you can
In the name of something 'new and grand.'

But as that Phoenix from the ashes lands,
So will Karma come back to man-
Disregarding Hearts of others
Is Disregarding that we're all brothers.

And in as much you've done to one-
In a matter of time,
Becomes Your Sun!

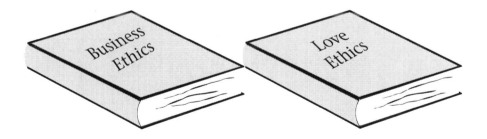

"The Bottom Line"

One of The Greatest Lessons
Taught me at the end-
When my Mother's body lessened
So Her Light could then Transcend....

Was Something she used to tell us
When Things went bad to worse-
You'll never see through all the dust
A U-Haul following a Hearse.

Focus on the 'Bottom Line'
And how much you can make,
Is Focus on what's gone in Time
On things you cannot take.

For the Only Thing you leave behind
Is what you Give to others:
Love and Joy and Memories Kind
And the Heart you give another

So next time you let your day be sad
By Business gods who hurt-
Remember When a Heart Departs,
No U-Haul Follows A Hearse!

"WWCJD"
(What Would Corporate Jesus Do?)

In The Land of Corporate America,
Decisions must be made:
Between The Growth in Greed they show-
Or Compassion being paid.

'Success' on Earth may be measured
At All Costs: "The Bottom Line" -
But Eternally what Heaven Treasures
Is What You Leave Inside-

The Love You Leave Behind.

"To The 'Dissed' "

So Here's The Deal:

It Doesn't Matter
If one dis-respects.
It says more about Them than You.
So Hold your Head High and Fly Above
When they act less than Truth.

Take The High Road-
Send More Light!
Send More When They Send Less.
Let No One hurt your Worthiness.
Take The High Road-
Live Your Best!

Live Love, Live Light, Live Blessed!

"When There's a Block on Your Yellow Brick Road"

And the Detour shined before her...
As if in The Land of Oz-
"The Grass is Always Greener"-
When the Familiar Turns
To Odd...

The Famous 'They' always say:
"Better not stay here too long!
Keep moving Up
When times get tough
They take for Granted Song!"

So on the Path to 'Higher Ground'
Detours caught her Eye
Stopped by unexpected Angels
And The Kindest Hearts that Shine!

When we want to Hurry to Higher Gates,
When Detours feel too long-
Hold On, as Higher Vision waits:
God Turns Right from Wrong-
Hold On, God Knows Your Song!

"Heavenly Road Blocks"

Are you Blocking Love Somewhere?
Holding Back in Anyway,
A Thought that's Kind, expressed with Care?
Putting Shade upon your day?

Did you know that when you Block
Anyone from your Heart,
You also Block The Master-
You Also Block HIS Love.

You can keep your 'Healthy Boundaries,'
If a negative vibe appears,
But never Block your Good Intent
To Send Love without fear.

So remember when you feel ANY
'Not So Positive' response,
Turn it Around to Higher Ground
And Save Your Soul With Love.

"At The End of The Race"

Reaching Great Accolades-
The Goal of Each Traveler here.
Excited to Win, it was God that would lend
The Final reward without Fear.

The Greatest Surprise at the end of her ride
Was not the Reward she expected-
It wasn't for running the fastest, the bestest -
It was Greater than All she Reflected!

It was about how she treated each one on the way-
From her helpers to those never knew
Were put in her Path, for a Much Greater Task
Of Seeing the 'Me' Inside 'You.'

Was she Kind? Was she giving while making her living?
Did she care for the others she knew?
At the End she would find Life's More Than a Line-
It's The Way You Live Wholly Love's Truth.

"The Road Peace Travels"

Whatever blocks your Total Peace-
Time to Let it Go...
Whatever makes your Dream Self cease-
Time to Change your Road.

It's Closer than the Air you Breathe,
The Elixir to discord.
Whoever turns your Soul to Grieve
Is furthest from your Lord.

See them Through Love's Eyes --
When Pain Of Blame seeps in your Heart-
And Right or Wrong, let Love replace
What judgment tears apart.

Whatever keeps you from your Peace-
Time to Let it Go...
And soon you'll find
The Power of Kind
Will Transform Every Woe.

The Path To Peace: Let Go!

When Seeking Solace in the world we live in:

"The Race for Grace"

This is for All
Unspoken Prayers
Unspoken worries
Unspoken Cares
That Unexplainable Uncertainty-
Not knowing Where
One's Heart may be.

This is for that weird Unknowing-
Concern just what Life
May be Showing...
When people change
Their moods and truths-
There's no control
What they say or do.

Be Brave Be Strong
Be Love Be Change-
Don't let low forces win.
To Change The World
The Change comes First
From The Power of Love Within.

One Voice-
Where Change Begins.

CONNIE FREEMAN PRINCE
"The Serpent & The Tree"

"Watch Your Back!"
Said the serpent, as it rolled around the Tree.
"I'm The One you're warned about-
Guaranteed to Take Your Peace!"

Listening through the Upper Branch,
An Angel perched above-
Could not help but over hear,
As Protection She's made of.

"Take Heed Tree, don't fear retreat-
As the Serpent circles round.
It knows your Roots run way too deep
To leave your Higher Ground.

Let your Stillness, Strong & Sure
Withstand the Serpent's plight.
For when it sees you Keep Your Peace,
Your appeal will leave Its sight.

The Only Thing to Watch instead,
Is Its mark upon your bark-
To tempt your Blame on others ways-
That it's 'Their Fault' of Heart.

As a Snake is just a Snake - no more.
It's You who give it Power-
Insisting hurt cut to your Core
Is the reason that you cower.

It may crawl around you-
But It Cannot Go Inside...
Unless you Let It ground you
With Its circling lies.

So Just Relax-
Sweet Tree of Life,
And know The Worst 'Attack'
Is The One in Closest Sight:
Ourselves - when we choose Lack.
God's Here - We've Got Your Back!"

"A Bump In The Road"

There's a Bump
There's a Bump
There's a Bump in the Road
Right when it seemed so smooth-
When there's Disrupt, It's then that we Must
Keep our Deep Souls On the Move!

There's a Path we must Trust -
In the Good and The Just.
Remember that Dragon's A Sign-
That You're So Close-
Don't Give Up -Keep Your Goals
It just means Your Dream's Here Right On Time.

The Gate Keeper's Beyond-
So Stay True to Your Bond-
Don't let it throw your Resolve.
Keep your Eye On The Prize
Let Your Greatest Self Rise-
This is Your time to Evolve!

SACRED SCARED

"The Sacred Scared"

When Scared - You've Cared,
Cared to Dare-
And Care's where Bravery's Found.
Not in the 'Safe' - No Chance to take,
But stayed on stable ground.

Time to shake the status quo
And scramble words around!
Turn Scared into Sacred Soul
Just switch the fear you found.

The Sacred's There, When Scared, So Dare!
Just look real close at Spelling:
Your Letters turned around with flair-
Is Where your Wisdom's Telling.....

"The Savior's Sand"

Ever been in 'Quick Sand?'
Not the kind down in the ground-
But the kind Inside where all Fears hide-
Where your Dreams begin to drown?

When you cannot Move your Body Up
Out Of Bed Sometimes.
When You cannot Do What you Love to Do,
Cause your Energy Resigns.

That's The Time to Go Within
And Breathe Inside Your Soul....
So Deep The Breath Of Life Comes In
To make your Heart Feel Whole.

That's The Time You Call Upon
The Reason You Are Here.
That's The Time-You Call Upon
Love's Presence Without Fear....

And Surrender To Your Higher Self
To Rise To Higher Land...
Let Go, Let God, Let All Be Well
On The Savior's Quick Soul Sand!

New Year Nudgings:
"The Roots Of Resolution"

"You Need A Goal!"
said Big Green Tree,
Towering over Tulip Plant.
"Spring will be here before you know
and you still can't even stand!"

So the Little Tulip pushed and pushed-
to be as 'Big' as Tree.
She wondered if her Worth was measured
by the Height another sees.

Until one day the Great Rains came
And she thought she'd drown for sure!
Her roots felt like they were digging deeper
instead of raising her.

So she gave up -- her drive was sunk
into a deep despair.
She thought she'd never Reach High Up
to the Tree's Success to Share.

Until one day her petals popped-
and stretched out on their own-
No one could even try to stop
her Destiny unfold.

And in Nature's Glory -- in due time --
She reached her Highest Goal.
She didn't even have to try-
just Be what's in her Soul.

The Tree is 'Famous' for its Height
But so's the Flower below.
Success is measured not by Sight
IT JUST IS -- When Allowed To Grow!

LET GO AND LIVE --

GOD KNOWS

"How To Change The World"

As a New Day Dawns,
'One Day at A Time' Certainly comes to mind
Before The Rest comes through your blinds-
Adjust Perception's Find:

Not the Screen you're looking at Reflecting Distant Minds,
But Clear The Lens the Camera sends Interpreting The Times.

If the Lens you look at Life through Is dusty with old dirt,
What you'll see is Not True- But a Reflection of the worst.

But if your Lens is Clear and Clean With no Past Refuge hurt,
You'll see Good and Bad More Clearly, add Interpretation's Worth.

But to Really Change the world you see,
Take the Youngest Mind you know -
And Protect Its Lens as Life Begins-
To Look through Love that Grows.

Before the outside world throws curves,
Before their Screen gets wild-
Let God's Love Be The First It's Heard-
And This World Will Change With A Child.

"Visitation"

There were dark souls all around her
Invading private Light
Seeping into her Consciousness
No Boundaries in sight.

She prayed for Strength to Rise Above,
With Peaceful Wings to Fly
But they found a way to bring her down-
Blindsiding every try.

She called upon High Spirits
To help her rise above-
For alone, Oh how she'd fear it -
All these claws disguised as love.

As they'd latch onto her Spirit Skin
And sucked out her very Life.
Where e'er she went she could not win
Each Joy gave way to strife.

I Want Out!
Her Soul would cry
I Want Out to Be!
Take me Out
Of these limited lies
I'll die if not set Free!

Surrounded by disguised false ties
She must escape this knot.
It's Time to Fly Above the cries
And Trust the God you've got ...!

Then as if by magic,
The web untangled free
And what she thought was tragic
Transformed to Light to See....

For often near a Breakthrough
The Darkness tries to fight
Only to birth a Morning
With the Gift of Life!

So...if you find yourself in Waters
That drown your dreams so deep:
Take Heart! Take Faith! Go Farther!
Let Angels help you leap.....

Up to a Higher Level
Where Perception can be seen -
From a Higher View from Heaven
It's Growth to Destiny!!

"The Re-Charge Rhyme"

An 'Extension Cord' to a Miracle
To plug into One Step Higher
We can't go back to the Umbilical -
One more slap for cryers.

Time to Breathe Into The Source
Plug into More than us
When winds try to blow us off The Course
And throw us under the bus.

Say Watt? What Watt? The Highest One-
With 24 Hour Light
For What's ahead seems dark at best -
So need more Light for Sight.

So Beam us Up, O Higher Cord-
Wake us Up Above!
When lost Today, Please Light Our Way
With Your Energy Saver: LOVE!

"Just Ask"

If you're In The Middle,
And Conflict begins to brew ...
-Just Ask Help for this Riddle
And It Will Be Solved For You.

If The Argument may Threaten
The Peace that you Breathe
-Just Ask- And Pray to Heaven
And Get Down On Your Knees.

.

No Storm is Too Threatening
No Time Too Unsettling
For God and His Angels Regime.

Their Wisdom's Always Waiting
For You -Yes - Just Saying,
They're There
To Help You Up That Slippery Stream

-Just Ask-
And Let Go.
-Just Ask -
Let Love Show
The Answer
When None's left to See.

And Breathe in The Peace
They have Waiting So Sweet
-Just Ask-
And With Trust:
LET IT BE.

"In Heaven's League"

A Little Rose -- plucked and planted
In a Smaller Field of Mums,
Was wondering if her position granted,
Was less powerful than some.

The Sun said, "Don't I Shine On You With
Equal Light each day?
What e'er The Garden,
God shows His Pardon
With His Own Eternal Pay:

There is no 'Big' or 'Little League'
In Heaven, Competings cease.
Your Worth is Given
By The LOVE You're Livin'-
In The Garden Of Eternal Peace.

120

"In Destiny's Flow"

As The Seed of The Rosebud -
Blooms When The Time Is Right...
So The Seed of Mankind -
Is at The Mercy of Nature's Might.

While Each Depends on A Higher Sight,
God Lead Us Gently Out of The Night.

Help Us Love and Not Fight Life.

Help Us Love and Reach New Heights!

Till The Time We Board Our Forever Flight!

GPS: "Guidance, Pray Soul"

Upon the Raft Of Reality
A Lifeboat swayed in the wind
Trying to find some Sanity
At Sea- Adrift -- Again....

Sent out Flares Up to the Sky
For Directions Up from Heaven
Praying Angels flying by
Take Heed, Advice Be Given....

Adrift in So Many Directions
Which to Choose To Start
Over with New Reflections
It's Nature's 'Come As You Are.'

So Many Dreams been put on Hold
A Holding Pattern it seems....
But know just Who is 'Holding' You
Is Bigger Than Your Dreams!

Hold On.... Press On....
BREATHE AND BE
One Step In Front of The Other....
And TRUST You Will Be Led to See
Your Destiny Uncovered!

"Good, Good, Good, Good Vibrations"

A Golden Vibe in The Universe,
Unseen by Blinded Souls,
Seemed Limited and Small At first-
Till She Chose to Raise her Goal...

To Rise Above an Ego Guard
In a Corporate world afraid,
Rise Vibrations High Above
So No Small Thought Invades!

Let not the Mediocre
Set your standards low-
Or interpret what you're here for,
When You Know Your Higher Goal.

So Shine Your Light Amidst The Dark!
Shine Light On All Closed Doors!
And Vibrate So, Your Soul Will Go
To The Place You Were Born For!

"Nature's Revolution"

The World Has Changed In Front Of Our Eyes-
More Obvious than Ever.
Sending Signs to Human Kind-
Unpredictable as The Weather.

But Now, our 'Weather' has Reached Inside-
So Much to Give us Pause-
Slowing Down our Rush to Ride
Uncertainties that Cause...

Undue Panic when Peace we need-
Undue Fear Precedes-
When we refuse to Live Beliefs
Of Higher Realms Unseen.

Time to Unwind All Mankind-
To Evaluate What's True...
What Really Matters as 'Reality' Scatters:
Do You Live The LOVE In You?

Slow Down...
And Live Your Truth!

"~~~ Wiggling In Your Chair Brain ~~~"

Restlessness is Labor Pains
Giving Birth to Thought-
Struggling to Break Free, Be Sane
In a world of chaos caught.

Let Give Birth to Higher Worth-
Never Stop Striving Higher.
But as you do, don't forget to brew
The PRESENT Sip Inspired!

"Winter Whimsies"

Accept the Heavenly Moments:
Warm Sunshine in the Cold...
Notice the Beauty of Shadows
As Sunshine turns to Gold.

Reminders to take off our Shades
Inside that dim our View
Of little bits of Heaven
God tries to show His Truth

As our furry friends bask in The Light
Rolling over in delight...
While Humans rush to one more crush
Blinded by their fights.

Breathe in This Day Of Nature's Way-
The Sunshine in the Cold
And take a Break for Heaven's Sake
What Glories to Behold!

And The Light said to The Darkness:
"Why are you still here?"

And The Darkness replied:
"How else could I see you?
Do you not shine Brighter in my presence?
Do I not give you the opportunity to show Who You Really Are?"

And The Light said:
" But with you comes such pain and sadness to those who view you."

And The Darkness said:
"Which is why You are still here.... I need you, too.
Without you, I would have no purpose."

The Light:
"But will my Children of Light ever get to experience
Only Light and No Pain?"

The Darkness:
"Only when they enter the place I cannot: Heaven.
But till then, It is I who Thank You
for showing them how to bring
Our Heaven
to Earth.
We are all Connected in our Lessons here.
Even You and I.
When My Darkness is viewed through Your Eyes of Light,
Heaven is found even here.
Which is why our Great Teacher taught us
to 'Love our Enemies'......
For what you put out into this world, is returned.
Which is why I secretly love and am grateful to you, Dear Light.

The Most Challenging Question now becomes:
Can you be Grateful to me?"

"And The Darkness Said Again ..."

"Why are you praying?
Don't you see that I'm still here?
I Still cover this world with heartache
I Still shower it in fear?"

And The Light replied:
"Ah, Darkness, my stubborn ageless friend,
As much as you may taunt and try-
My Faith Will Never End ....

If you could See What I See,
You'd see More Than What You Do:
The Stars in the Night
The Light of the Moon
There's Also Light In You!

I choose to see The Light In You
Which is Not an easy Truth
But there's Still a Star
There's Still a Moon-
Depending On Your View:

The Darkest Night gives Rise to Morn
Such is The Cycle of Life
But till it does, a Star is Lit
To Light your way through Night.

So Bright The Sun Still chooses to Rise
Like Clockwork- God's Work- Untorn.
It's a Life of Resurrection Signs,
To Heal what makes forlorn.

As Nature teaches in our Passage
Through our Paths through Time...
God's Trust securely never breaches
Even when our own declines.

Light in The Darkness - The Stars in The Night
Must Still Run Into Sun To Brighten our Sight.
We each Choose to See The Darkness or The Light.
So, Why do we Pray? To Purify Sight...

Purify, Clarify - Perceive from Above:
Look Up, in Times Tough -- Find Light, Lense of Love."

"Looking Through God's Glasses"

If I could LIVE Through YOUR Eyes,
What kind of world would it be?
If I could See Through Dis-guise,
Would I See What You Would See?

Beneath all anger and ego despair,
Would I See No Danger?
Would I See Your Care?
Would I See There Really Are No Strangers-
When Connecting Love That Shares...

Just Growing Souls, in Search Of Peace-
In Search Of Love's Arranger...
We have an Inner Child who Pleads
To See His Holy Manger.

Let Us Look Through Your Kind Eyes-
Let Us See What You Would See-
Let Us Live Beyond Our Minds.
Let Us Live In Love Through Thee.

"On Earth As Heaven Is"

In a world of scattered strife,
There lives a Place Inside
That knows What's Wrong - and knows What's Right-
A Place we can confide.....

Silence All-
And Go Within.
Ask for Guidance-
Let Your Savior In.

Heaven is Closer than you think...
It just takes Focus
To find Its Link:

Be Kindness, Be Love.
Let The Opening Start-
The Path To Heaven
Begins In Your Heart.

129

"The Unveiling"

Love is in The Details-
Ask any Flower that blooms-
God's Potpourri Of Retail-
So much He must find Room...

Creating from His Vision,
He knows His End Result-
For Creating With Precision
Is what makes our world so full.

Rich In Vibrant Color-
Each Texture Deep and Grand.
Though to grow, we suffer
The Detailed Growing Man.

Love is in The Details
As He Knows Behind Each View-
You must allow Time Unveil-
His Patient Path to Truth.

"Love Is In The Details...."

The Crux Of Creation's Art:
The Tiny Fur on a Kitten's Tail-
The Bee's Wing That travel's Far...
The Deep Red Color in a Rose's Petal-
The Tall Tree That Rises Far.....

The Grin On a Baby's Innocent Face
The Butterfly who cannot Settle
The Leaf falling softly into place.
The Invisible Breeze so gentle....

Inside the Smallest Detail -
From Ants and All Cliches,
The Greatest Detail God Displays Is:
Who YOU Are Today!

Dance! You're In His Play!

"Are You Lacking?"

Whenever you feel a Lack with Someone-
Look at the Lack within Yourself.
For Everything's a Reflection Of
You In Someone Else.

Whenever you Feel 'left out' -
With those who you thought were close,
Remember to Respect the Best In All-
What e'er the popular hosts....

It's All Okay- All leads The Way-
To your Higher Self You Be.
Breathe In Each Moment
Transcend and Go In...
And Be What You're Meant to Be.

Fill your Soul
And Live, Be Whole.
Be what you Dreamed.
Be Peace.

"The Light House"

When Life's Waves Feel Overwhelming -
With your mere body as your Raft,
With cries for Help surrounding-
Floating Up- a daunting task.

That's when you Look to 'The Light House'...
Let Its Beams Bathe Deep Your Soul.
That's One Place Light Will Ne'er Go Out-
No task too great Its toll.

Follow that Light!
Can You See It?
It takes Focus - Inside Sight.
To see You ARE The Light House.
God Built You through the Night.

So when those waves crash all around you-
Climb Up In Consciousness ...
And Know Your Captain and Your Crew
Are The Light Of Righteousness.

Breathe Deep His Promises.
You're His House Where Angels Rest.
Hold On. Be Strong.
Be Blessed.

"....and then came The News Again"

To a Speechless Sequel,
Where Hurt Unequals,
I tried to write for You
A Heartfelt Prayer in Deepest Care
Where Tragedy renews....

And Strikes right through your Tender Heart.
Dear God we Pray to You
For Guidance, as we've never prayed-
Help those in Search for Truth.

Let not more shots ring silence
To Moral Laws ignored.
Guide our Leaders Action Take
Guide Us when we are torn.
-
Let not Insanity re-make
New 'Normals' horror view.
How to deal with Heartless Souls
Lost in hate pursued.

How to comfort Innocence
When No Words make it Well.
May The Miracle of Enough Great Souls
Re-write this Path to Hell.

Out Number those so lost in pain-
Take back our Country's Conscience sane.
With the Price of Human Cost.
Keep Hope Alive When We Feel Lost.

"Got News?"

Don't allow Them to get into your Head-
You have more Power than you think.
Don't allow your Soul be led-
By the lowest in the rink.

Let them skate around you,
But not in your Circle of Truth.
Your Sacred Space Inside You
Creates Your Greatest View.

"Tourniquet For the Politically Wounded"

Make It STOP
The Human Suffering
Make It STOP
Before It Begins
Make It STOP
The Sane who Choose its Buffering
By Not Facing What They Defend.

What's More Important
When passing Laws:
Protection or Personal Gain?
What's More Important
When Human Flaws
Express Violent Ways AGAIN!?

Make It STOP
As God has Mercy,
He Gave The Power To Us...
Risk Self-Interest Controversy.
Bring Back:
In God We Trust!

"Love Letter for the Loveless"

To that Place Within your Heart-
Where you feel you've been betrayed,
To That Pain- Cuts Who You Are,
Time to See What God has made:

To replace that Spec of Dis-Respect,
So obvious by deed,
God's Angels send what you'll ne'er regret:
A New Place for You To Be...

In This New Place of Faith and Grace,
You'll Be Better Than Before-
But only If you can Forgive,
'Let Live' - Let Go Closed Doors.

Bless the Peeps who seemed 'asleep'-
They were playing out their parts...
Of Destiny that seemed to weep-
To Fine Tune your New Star!

So Bless The Process!
Bless The Souls-
Bless even those who smirk:
For in the end, The Pure Heart Wins-
Prepared to Do God's Work.

"Winner Winner Chicken Dinner??"

"Mega Chickie Dreams"

"So Chicken Little, Did You Win??"
Asked Miss Lillian when Lots were cast.
"Well, I'm not sure," he did begin,
"I don't count Chickens before they Hatch!"

"Then What Do you Count, if not the numbers
That didn't add up last night?"
"Well, I started with my Blessings-
Way over a Billion in sight!"

"Could a Win even Begin-To add to your 'Happy?'
Can It be measured in merely a Guess?

Could you buy True Love?
Could you buy True Peace?
Could you buy what truly lasts?"

"Why would I try? I already Have those 'things' -
And didn't even have to ask!"
"Then you Must have won the Biggest Lottery
That Ever crossed our laps!

Christ In Your Heart where True Riches Are-
The Greatest Gift You Will Find!
So Chicken Little, You're A Winner!
Winner Winner, Chicken Dinner!
You're a Winner, One of a Kind!

As is All your Friends and Nestings...
Living as A Spirit Giver
With Love & Chickie Blessings!!"
You Already are a Lottery Winner!

(Chicken Little Jr's Mega Lottery Adventure: "Before & After")

"A bell's not a bell 'til you ring it, A song's not a song 'til you sing it,
Love in your heart wasn't put there to stay, Love isn't love 'til you
give it away!" -- Oscar Hammerstein II

"Mis-Placed Giving"

When you Give Away What's In Your Soul:
Momentos, Thoughtful Things,
Do you ever feel it takes a toll
From what your Spirit brings?

If a twinge of guilt becomes too real,
Think where that may come from-
Are you putting mis-placed Value on
What others know not of?

Don't you see it doesn't matter-
The 'Thing' you give at all-
Its Essence never can be measured,
For Its Purpose Transcends All...

When Given from your Soul Intent
Of Helping Heal One's Heart,
Then know Its Purpose-
Divinely Sent-

Is God's Love Through Who You Are.
It's The Messenger playing His Part.
It's The Love True Giving Imparts.
Giving's Where Blessings Start.

"Stretching Signs For Healing Times"

Out from the Walls
Of Hospital bare
Into the Green
We're walking Out There…

In overwhelmed numbness
Of shared Overload-
Our Feelings of Oneness
Have forced us to Grow.

Hand in Hand, in slow gait,
Needing Faith, while we wait-
More 'forms' we must fill out -
Praying "God Help Us Be more Filled with Your Strength!"
One more Round, So Raw we could shout!

We walked outside to a Sunlit Day
After Hours of cool steel-
Relieved to see some Sun our way-
Calm Moments as these we steal.

My Beloved looks down the sidewalk-
We notice One Flower Alone-
The Brightest of Yellow, it seemed to Talk-
Its Roots through Concrete had grown…..

And though surrounded by unnatural land,
It somehow managed to Stand-
To Greet mere humans as us unassumin'
With wonder if This God Had Planned...

For these bodies imperfect:
Our Gifts to Garage
Our Souls on this earth
In this Life, a Mirage.

This little Dandelion
Yelling out without tryin,'
Its Yellow Sang a silent Hello!
A Sign! I mused to my Beloved to use,
Even Nature seeks Truth when It Grows.

So to you on Your Path, whether Flower or Human,
May we All find in passing, what Lasts.
As our Time is Illumined by These Moments Pursuin'
Peace when we feel our lots cast.

Life gets our Attention
The most surprising of ways.
Even the smallest of Nature-
Stretches to Pray.

"Like a Boat Over Troubled Waters..."

The waves came crashing round us.
Intense, yet kissed with Son -
The Son of God's Bright Promise,
His Miracle's Begun...

So Sail we are amidst the currents
Of uncertainty's fierce roar.
Sail we are when over our heads
In waters way from shore.

As a Human holding the paddle
To keep on course this Boat,
It feels as if it's drowning-
No choice but Keep Afloat.

Nauseous Tired Exhausted.
The paddle heavy held -
But when it's on Your Shoulders,
No choice but Hold The Helm.

The One Who Walked On Water,
Please take this oar from me.
But my Soul could never leave this boat,
For it carries Soul Mate sweet.

Help me God - Please make me Strong
And Well to make the shore.
A Miracle we pray for Health-
When feeling Less, You're More!

"God's Safety Tips"

When it's hard to do Life's Heavy Lifting,
Look for The Leverage Of Love...
Bend your knees,
Lift Through the Trees-
Pray Up To Help Above...

Focus on The Higher Realm-
Look Up to The Highest Shelf.
Tune into Who Is at your Helm-
And Lift Up To Your Best Self!

Lift High- Lift Deep- Breathe Well!

God's Angels Live To Help!

"Gone...Fishing"

A Survival Story For The Creative Soul

"Do you like the Bowl you're Swimming in?"
Asked the Angel to the Fish.
"Do you know my cries," the Fish replied,
"For Higher Waves, I Wish?"

"I can sense your deep frustration,
As you yearn for Higher Realms,
And was sent for your Vibration-
To help Raise to Higher Helms."

"What's wrong with my Vibration?"
Asked Little Fish, So meek.
Then the Angel brought her Revelation-
The Answer Fish did seek:

"Begin to Swim 'As If' You Swam
In the Ocean your Soul Craves...
Catch the Waves of Your "I Am":
"I Am" my Higher Waves!"

"I AM" I BREATHE! I LIVE The Seas
Where my Dream Thoughts wish to Be..."
And soon you'll Become What You See-
Your Higher Form Of 'Me!'

Then soon her small Vibration Grew
So High, she Flew Way Up-
And landed on a Raindrop
That landed on a Cup.

The Cup picked Up by A Prophet's Soul,
Aquarium's dear Friend,
And shone her as a Gift Of Gold
So Bright her Light did lend!

They found a Special Place for her-
Riding waves So Bold!
All because she BECAME The Wave
That pushed her out of her Bowl!

Vibration Leads To Growth and Flight -
To Light -- Our Ultimate Goal...
But First The LIGHT must BE our Sight-
To Free Our Creative Soul!

LIVE Your Truth-
Be Whole.

The Red Leaf in Summer
("The Leaf Who Lost Her Season")

On the Hottest Day of Summer
The Lush and Green In Bloom,
A displaced Leaf ducked under
The Green to find some room.

She blushed with Red when a cooler spell
Came through the first of Spring
And got confused which season fell
As her Color lost its zing!

She hung on there through storms and nights-
A First for her plant kind.
Am I too late? She asked with fright!
Just waiting for her sign.....

Should she 'fall' or should she 'stay'?
For already friends she'd made
With the other leaves who liked her way
Of complimenting shade.

So living outside her Comfort Zone
Wasn't odd at all.
It didn't matter the color grown
Through Summer, Spring or Fall!

And then the thought occurred to me
Admiring her Courage to Live,
Among Different Leaves, Accepting These
If only We All Could Give....

Acceptance through Whatever Season
God changes us to bear-
We could learn from Nature's Reason
All Life Is Here To Share!

"One Change"

If WE ALL Just Took A Moment -
This Moment - Right Now:
And sent Loving Healing Light To ALL
We'd Feel Love Hug All Around...

The Energy would Impact-
In a Prayer that Love would send...
And Cause The Greatest Re-Act
Of Peace that would not end.

But it takes us ALL to join as One
To Remember Who We Are:
God's Hands and Feet and Daughters and Sons
A Part of Every Star.

A Hurricane Of Love to sweep
All Hate to be unfurled...
Begins with Trust Inside Of Us:
God's Love To Change The World.

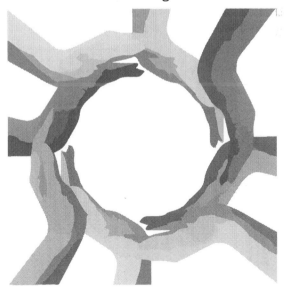

This Poem was written for The Dedication of "The Garden Of Peace" in Jackson, Tennessee.

The Special Garden now lives on Peacefully, surrounded by a Beautiful Angel now standing on the property of The Therapy and Learning Center. Numerous names of sweet children and Souls are subscribed upon it, who now reside with her in Heaven.

It was her Dream to see this Dedication before her passing. But Heaven called her Home several months Before. Thanks to the generosity of the West Tennessee Healthcare Foundation, my wonderful Nephews Brad and Stephen Little, my sweet siblings, and many caring Spirits at who loved her so much in Jackson, her Dream Did become a Reality.

I wrote this in Honor of my Mother and All of "God's Special Children," as she would so lovingly call them, on the many years she helped raise money for children with Cerebral Palsy on their yearly Telethons. You can read about her Special Influence in all of our lives in our Thanks and Acknowledgments. This One's for you, Mama. Our Eternal Dedication.....

> "Welcome Home, Dear Garden of Peace,"
> Where God's Special Children Smile
> And Welcome Angels to this Ground
> So Close to Heaven's Sound...
>
> Welcome Home to our sweet Mother
> And Every Body's 'Cousin,'
> For all the times you'd sit and Pray
> For your Mission Complete with others.
>
> Now Rest Your Place of countless hours,
> Praying for those you Love-
> Re-United Now with Power
> That we on earth Dream Of!
>
> Today in Gratitude we see
> Angels from Above
> Long Live Our Mother's Garden of Peace-
> Back Home where you came from....
> Your Legacy of Love!

"Evolution"

We're Born to Die?
To say Goodbye
From our First to our Last Breath...
What Happens In Between's called 'Life'-
And "Death" is earned Blessed Rest.

Each Moment's Gone-
As it's Begun-
Must Notice each quick turn.
To Slow Down the Rush,
We First Must Hush-
Be Present Here To Learn...

We're Born to Cry-
To Laugh- To Sigh
To Feel and Think and Be-
Be Born To Fly
As Time Chimes By-
No End To You and Me...

Recycling All we See-
Into Eternity...

"Of The Sacred Breath"

If we could grasp The Sacredness
In the Smallest Breath unheard...
The Beauty Of The Grandest Star
That never says a word-

If we could Feel the Magnitude
Of The Universe's Care-
Perhaps Then we'd finally learn
God's Depths Of Love We Share...

Life's Sacred Every Where,

With Joy, No Fear Can Bear,

Transcend- Fall Into Prayer.

Hope Springs When We're Aware.

"The Gift of Conscious Awareness"

If you only knew ....

My Deepest Wish Is That You Remember...

How Very SACRED Every Moment
of Every Day IS that you are on this earth -
To forming Your Destiny Beyond-
Mediocrity would no longer be fatigue's default reaction.
Every Encounter, Every Happening
(from joys to disagreements)
would be Consciously Considered....

As a falling leaf tumbling to its ground,

A drop of rain Dancing upon your crown,

A Prayer pondering every forgotten frown.

The Art of Life is In Its Turnaround.

The Gift of 'Imperfect Peace'

'Twas time to put the rest away-
Clearing out the past...
Getting ready for this New Year
Sweet cards whose memories last.

One we've kept Year after Year
With the Simple Letters 'PEACE'
Withstanding spills, some tears appeared
And at first I felt dis-ease.

How can this Lovely symbol 'Peace'
Once white & pure & clean
Be kept displayed with Letters frayed
What could its meaning be?

And then I looked again its frame
Once perfectly untouched-
And realized its Beauty came
From Its Symbol, not its rust.

Earthly things may come and go
Not lasting the harsh of time,
But what they stand for always shows
A Beauty that Still Shines!

So when earthly treasures show their wear
And tear from being alive,
Just know their imperfection
Adds Character that thrives...

And now when I look at my slightly rumpled
Sign which spells out 'PEACE'
I'll remember 'Peace' remains unruffled
Beneath what Mankind Sees.

CONNIE FREEMAN PRINCE

"The Fight for Flight"

I Fought Change -
Till....
A Butterfly Dared To Break Out Of Cocoon-
Showing the Beauty
Of Courage To Move.

And The Falling New Snow Of A Long Winter's Blues-
Gave Birth to New Life-
Sharing Springtime's Perfume.

I Fought Time -
Till .....
It helped my past Broken Heart to Mend.
As I Breathed In The Moment
God's Mercy Transcends.

I Fought Forgiveness -
Till....
I Learned 'Being Right' held Me back from my Peace-
And Hurt So Much More Than 'Being Happy' as Me.

I Fought Life-
Till...
I Learned
Changing Times And Forgiveness
Are The Keys To True Peace
To unlock A Blocked Heart-
When No Peace We Can See.

I Found Love-
When...
I Let Life's Keys
Break Open My Heart-
To Embrace Every Second-
To Light Who We Are...

And There -
I Found God.

154

-- Defy the Fear of Being Alive --

Dare To Rise Dare To Fly!

"CHANGES"

What Is Life, but Changes?
Like Summer Into Fall
Like Winter Re-Arranges
Its barren trees to Call...
For Spring Time's Promised Beauty
Just waiting Time to Dance
Into Its Sacred Duty
To Deliver Hope in Chance...
So Take a Chance and Change and Dance-
Become All You're Meant To Be!
And as in Nature, you'll Advance
Into Your Own Destiny!

In Honor of our Ever Evolving Friends on This Journey!

"A Call to Angel Arms"

Explosions in the Galaxy
Put Angels on Alert -
Mis-Guided leading travesty
Not aware of those who hurt.

How to put the fires out
That Unconsciousness slow burns...
How to help The Soul Shouts
Of a Democracy once heard.....

Dear God we pray for a Miracle
In our Country today.
Open the Minds of the cynical
Open the Hearts of the crazed.

Give Guidance to the Peacemakers
For Laws of Peace to stand.
Protect their Rights with no more fights
Bring Sanity to This Land!

Dear God We Pray for a Miracle-
Correct these errored days.
Dear God We Pray for a Miracle-
Direct our Leader's Ways!

Light Unite!

Calling All Light Workers!

Beings of The Light

In times of unhealed furor

It's Time to Be In Sight...

Blind, the misled on the side
Of racists led by hate.
With So Much Light - God Clear their Sight
To see Love cannot wait...

We cannot wait for Peace to Be
It's We who hold The Key-
By Living In Love Energy
That spreads from sea to sea...

Calling All Light Workers!

Don't discount Today-

The slightest sight of furor-

Heals When We ALL Pray

"Lit from Within"

She looked outside and couldn't see
As Darkness fell so scarily
All around the world it seemed
Shadows shading Clarity.

Where Is The Light to Shine upon?
The Guide to notice right from wrong?
It seems the world forgot the song
Of Harmony to get along.....

So as she prayed all night and day
Trying to figure out the play
She felt a nudge Inside that came-
From a Place that had no name.

And then a Light Bulb o'er her head
Said "Look Up! It's Time! Rise from the dead!"
But first to See, you first must try
To Open Wide Your Own Eyes!

There is no Light Outside to find
If you cannot see from Light Inside
To change the outside screen so mean
You first must change the Lens you dreamed.

There is No Light to recognize
If you cannot See from Open Eyes-
But The Only Eyes that can Transcend
Are the ones that Look Through LIGHT Within.

Open Minds Help Eyes Transcend....
Speak Your Truth
From The Well Within

"In The Karmic Garden"

A Tender Hearted Flower
Crushed by the Twine near by,
Breathed In A Gentle Sweeping Breeze -
To Soothe what seemed Unkind.

The Twine had no idea it Strangled
All The Hope She Had-
For in that particular garden,
They Both Gave All They Had.

So the Flower Reached a Little Higher,
As the Twine curled further down.
Till a Forgiving Hand reached down to Plant
New Hope for Higher Ground.

As the Twine kept curling further down,
The Flower Then Forgave-
Realizing Her Soul Was Rising
In The New Ground God Had Paved.

In God's Garden, HOPE, Is Raised!

I Wish I May I Wish I Might
Be The Heart when Hearts hold Fright-
Be The Change in a World Of Tears
Be Why God Brought My Spirit Here.
This is The Story of A Wishing Well
A Story of Love and Prayer.
This is The Story I Live To Tell
In Gratitude for Souls Who Care.

"Miss Lillian's Wishing Well"

This is The Story of a Wishing Well
Where Thousands of Wishes Made
Represent Prayers and Cares
Of Young and Old who came....

Years and Generations
Shared their Family Dreams:
Births and Deaths and Children's Breaths
Poured into Its Stream...

Pennies brought from All our Guests
Given to me Here
To Give and Pray and Celebrate
Our Sharing through their years:

A young boy, now a Soldier,
Saved pennies every day
To Thank us All, for All he's fought-
Growing up at 'Miss Lilly's.'

A Widower saved His Wife's Penny
For her Tombstone.
And to this day, comes back to pray
So he won't feel so alone.

A young Mother did hesitate
When Its Power became known-
When her young son, wished for a Brother-
And now he's almost grown!

Years of Wishes
Prayers and Kisses
Chickie Blessings
Smiles and Songs
If you could see the faces sweet
You'd know these Feelings Strong.

Now for the Pennies I still have left,
Entrusted to my care-
From many who grew up here
Who Asked I give and share...

I throw them in and Give Them
I throw them from my Heart.
Through Years and Tears and Joys and Fears
We've ALL been through A Lot!

Times may Change and Re-Arrange-
But One Thing I pray Time Tells:
The Memories and Wishes Made
In "Miss Lillian's Blessing Well."

"Morning Prayers
For Those Who Care"

"What Would You Have Me Do Today?
Who Would You Have Me See?
In a world of unknown plays,
How Would You Have Us Be?"

As the 'Son' Rises With Us,
Help Us Rise to Greater Scenes...
Remembering Nothing's Greater
Than Seeing the 'You' in 'Me.'
He Lives In All We See.
Help us Breathe This Day In Thee.

"Prayers From The Rear View Mirror"

Dear God,

Help me Forgive the Blocks I thought
Came from Another's Hands-
Help me React with Kindness taught
When Judgment takes a stand.

Help me remember that No One Person,
Company or Man-
Can take Away Your Purpose -
Can take away Your Plan!

So while the chips fall where they may...
And Circumstances Be-
Help me, God, Just See Your Way
Your Love, Your Destiny...

To remember what I see in another-
Also comes from me-
Do I want to be 'Right' even when it smothers
My Path to Inner Peace?

Help me see Only Through Your Eyes
And with Your Wisdom see:
That The Only Way to Rise Up High
Is when Praying on my knees.

Dear God, Please Live Through me.

"Prayers for Comfort"

Prayers for Comfort
Prayers for Peace
Prayers all Under
Our Prayers ne'er cease.

When feeling helpless
We'll Hold On To Each Other
When feeling distress
We remember to cover...

Our Hearts in The Breath
Of Hope we Inhale
Transcending All death
His Promise Prevail.

Help us to Breathe In this day
Help Help to find Its Way-
To All Who Need Us All to Pray
Our Hearts Are With You- You'll Be Okay!

"Prayer Purell"

Wash Over Me, Holy Light Of Love...
Cleanse Me, Heal Me Free!
Transform My Life Below-Above-
Pure Consciousness, Be Me.

Breathe Deep
Breathe Clean
Breathe Thee.

"When Prayer Requires An Inhale"

This is a Prayer for Healing
For All Fears Great and Small
For No Fear is so Small That Feeling
Fear can't make you fall.

What e'er your need for Healing Be
For You, Or One You Love:
I join with you, Connecting To
God's Power Inside....Above!

"Prayer for Transcendence"

Dear God, I Surrender
My Destiny To You.
Transform All My Thoughts
Into Your Words Of Truth.

Instill in Each Memory I leave on this earth
Into Just Joy, Just Love and Your Mirth

Make me an Instrument to Make Peace where there's pain.
Make every Incident into a chance to Reframe ...

All into Purity - Free from disdain.
Instill in each Memory
The Reason You Came.

Transform All my Energy
To Live In Your Name.

"Silent Company"

In The Silence
Do you Hear it?
The Undercurrents of Life....
In The Silence
Do you Feel it?
Your Mind massaged in Light...

Angel Wings in Silence
Make the Deepest Sounds
Angel Wings In Silence
Comb and Calm our Ground.

In The Silence
Take a Moment
Breathe and Breathe Again
For in These Moments
Without Earth knowin'
You'll Feel a Heavenly Friend.

A Quiet Break for your Day:

"Silent Song"

Silence woke with me Today...
And Bathed my Ears with Peace.
Silence spoke with me Today....
And Made my Soul at Ease.
Releasing Healing to All Around me
Increased my Peace Within-
Reminding me how it Astounds me
How Deep His Presence Is.
Silence Spoke to me Today.
I'm So Grateful that I Listened

"Interpretive Chance"

A Simple Little Branch-
Swept ashore from Storm...
The Wind swept up
To a sandy shore.

One passerby saw it
And Thought it an 'eyesore'-
Messing up where they sit-
Messing up 'sandy floor!'

Some ignored and some tripped over-
But Neutral it still stayed.
Waiting Interpretation of
Its New Purpose in the shade.

Till a little child ran to it-
And Its Purpose quickly changed:
Her Imagination invented
A Magic Wand That Played!

She Picked up the Stick
And began to draw a Heart into the sand
Her Joy transformed the 'eyesore'
Into a Loving Land...

Whatever Job you're given,
Is Neutral what it means.
You're given a Choice to live it
As a Joy or drudgery.

The Energy of Interpretation
Is Truly in Your Hands.
No stick is just a 'stick'-
When put into Creative Hands.

It depends on Where Perception may land....
...So God Created 'Man.'
To Make Life What You Can!

To An Anonymous Angel

Angels Earn Their Wings
In a Variety of Ways-
But I think the way of Holy Play
Is the Kind Who Leave No Name....

Like the One Who picked up lunch today
When we went to pay-
And were told The Ones ahead of us
Already Kindly Gave!

The Kindness of the Every Day
Is Angel Work on earth.
No need for Higher Accolades
When God knows your Real Worth.

So to our Angels with No Name-
Who Give no bow to Fame,
Thanks for Living God's Reward:
The Gift of Heaven's Gain.

"Angels Who Have Heard On High"

Angels Hear From Everywhere
Overtime these days-
Overwhelmed by Human Cares
And Hover Hurricanes....

Flooded with the drowning cries
Louder with each storm,
The loudest from the winded sighs
Of Human Hearts so torn.

So They Asked Their Angel Father
To send more Help to Earth
For They couldn't see much farther
With so much Human Hurt.

Then He Relieved and Gave Reprieve-
Reminding Who They Were:
Messengers To Help Them See
To Teach Them of Their Worth:

"I Gave Them Hearts for Reasons
I Gave Them Hands for Cause
I Gave Them Each New Seasons
To Apply Them All...

The Strength, The Power, the Help They Need?
Learned From Prayers They Bring...
As Angels High help plant the Seeds-
For Man To Earn His Wings."

169

"God's Engine Light"

A Simple Day of the Every Day
On this Healing Path we're on...
Turned out to not be O So 'Simple'
In Its Message come upon.

The last thing that we needed
Was an Engine Light come on-
To warn us needed checking
Inconvenience had begun.

So early in the next morn,
We took our poor car in.
And prayed that it would not be worn-
Have Mercy Mechanic Friend!

Another expense we did not need,
But with all the Prayer we've had-
We had to Trust that help we'd meet
That Good would come from 'Bad.'

Not sure if they could take us
With a parking lot so full.
But they did not forsake us
They said "Relax" (Remarkable!)

Then as we sat in the waiting room
In walked an interesting pair-
A man and wife who brought a Light
Of Joy, and not despair.

As pleasantries were exchanged
'Remarkable' explained-
That THEY had lives that were arranged
With Treatments they've maintained.

They had been to THE same places
That we had recently-
The same sweet nursing, caring faces
That helped us peacefully.

We shared 'Angel' stories
Of how They have appeared
To Bless us Both, on this Healing Boat
From the Cancer we have feared.

Though in outer looks, we were different books
From different backgrounds be -
But as we shared, our Souls were hooked In Familiarity.

The Gentleman in the shop came over
And said, "Here are your keys...
There's nothing wrong, to your engine's throng
No Charge, there are no fees."

The Engine Light that brought us there
Seemed another Purpose be -
Divine Timing caught unaware
To share our Prayers and See.....

That whenever 'Things Appear Go Wrong'
It is We who judge what seem
An Inconvenience to our daily song
Is Often Meant To Be.

God wakes us up from our routines
Of the every day
To remind us to pay attention, please,
To the Results from which we Pray.

Answers come in many forms
At unexpected times
So when your 'Engine Light' forewarns
Pay Attention to Its Sign....

Signs are EVERYWHERE on earth
Be glad when things shake up...
For it could be sent from Help Unheard
To Show Us We Are Loved!

171

"Message from A Fallen Angel"

A Porcelain Angel, commissioned to Sit
Upon a Sill, a window to lift-
Spent years with Care, her arm Raised Up,
Blowing a Kiss - Sending Her Love ...

Until one day, through no fault of her own,
She slipped and fell from off of her Throne ...
Her Arm flew down, straight to the ground
Unable to send her Love all around.

Her Human summoned to look after her too
Saw her dilemma, and just what to do ...
So she got out her glasses and True Super Glue
To Put back the Pieces, So Loving and True.

One couldn't tell looking at Her again
That a few hours ago, her Wing needed mend-
The Only Clue, of Imperfectitude
Was a slight little edge where the mending pursued.

Her Scar only Strengthened Her Arm's Holy Mission
Of Sending Pure Love, Through ALL ...
Lending us Lessons, Enduring Life's Questions:
'Perfection?' Even Angels Can Fall?

As Life Shakes Us Up, Even Wings go Kaput
But Still leave examples along-
That Truly, Falls That Don't Kill You,
Can Remarkably Leave You
Not shattered, but Even More Strong!

"Awakening"

Angels come in the middle of the night
To Hug your Gentle Soul
But you can't feel their quiet flight
When human angst unfolds.

Clear the Blocks of Love's Sweet Presence
By Forgiving, Letting Go...
Look at past hurts Differently -
Let Compassion be your Goal.

And in that Clear New View of All,
You'll Hear the Angels Call.
And wake you to a Brand New Morning
Of Peace Inside Your Soul.

173

"The 'Joy' Dilemma"

A little cloud on a stormy day
A strange dilemma saw
Living in the Eye of a Hurricane
In the midst of cries, felt Calm.

But How could there be Joy and Cries
Right at the very same time?
How could even Sense one find
In Such terrible earthly Signs?

Life is a paradox of Feeling
Changing with the Wind
A Brand New Child sends All Hearts Reeling
When New Life Begins Again!

Life's a Mixture, my Friend!

Ever feel like saying, "Stop the World, I Wanta Get Off?"

This Poem's For You.

"Break Dancing"

As the World is Spinning 'round us,
May our Souls Spin to Its Center-
Into a Sacred Place of Stillness
And Allow Pure Peace to Enter.

Stop.

Breathe.

Slow Down The Rush.

Breathe Deep.

Let This 'Now' Enter,
And Find Your Power
Transcend This Hour-
Dig Deep and Find your Center.

Exhale Peace
And Then Release
All Up To Higher Hands...
Then Spin Back Into This World
From The Center where Love Lands.
From That Place,
Take A Stand.

Come Back-
God Still Has Plans!
Joy Still Lives In Man.

"Surrender"

When you've Stood Up-
And Spoken Up-
From your Heart
And can't get through--
Sometimes just 'Letting Go' -
Is the hardest thing to do.

But you can't control another's Soul,
And their Point Of View.
Sometimes you can only Pray This Day
You Can Live In Your Own Truth.

Make Peace Inside of You
Let Go, Let God Make New...

To The Great Corrector,
And Life Protector,
Heal we pray All Loss.
Help us know You're THE Connector
To The Greater Good we've sought.

Rise Above What Can't Be Fought.
Experience Can't Be Taught.

"Surrender Dorothy!"

Forces Wrote
>Upon the Skies of Soul
>>Yet on her Journey into Oz
>>>Love: Her Only Goal.

>>>Still she had to battle
>>Flying monkey brains
>Who tried to shake her Faith and Rattle

The Reason Why She Came.

No matter what is in your Heart
>On your Journey here,
>>The Purest of Intentions part
>>>Interpreted through fear.

>>>So Hold Onto your Soul Slippers
>>When you step through Witch's Land.
>And don't let scary scissors

Rip apart God's Plan.

It's just a Sign you're making a Difference
>When Outside Forces Note
>>That your Life has Greater Reference
>>>Than what the Passive wrote...

>>>For on your Journey down that Road
>>You have to risk a fall -
>The Only Way to Reach a Goal

Is to Share It All...

It's often scary to share your Heart
>In a world of Heartless Souls.
>>But Remember God Made Who You Are:
>>Surrender to Love's Goal!

"In the Off Season"

A Lovely Little Flower
Peaked out of its Winter Sleep
Thinking In confusion
"Is Spring at Winter's feet?"

"You're not 'supposed' to Bloom In this!"
Her Mother Nature taught-
"And if too soon, a Bloom you'll miss
When the snow comes back to taunt."

So she bowed her head and felt so sad
Cause her Spring Inside still stirred
Yet feared if she jumped from her bed
The Garden might be hurt.

But the thought of feeling stifled
Out weighed the fear of Bloom
So she raised her head and Danced instead -
Wrong Season? Hey, Make Room!

And the Joy she felt
Stretching out her svelte
Petals, though half baked too-
Far surpassed the Aftermath
Of any 'Off Season' boo.

Then as her quick lived season
Began to feel the Cool,
It did remind twas time to wind
Back down to ground cocoon.

But before her Bloom went under,
Once again to bow to fate,
She noticed a Face of Wonder
Looking through her Garden Gate.

It appeared a 'Seasoned' Human
Many years beyond her prime
Realized She'd been assumin'
No more Springtime She would find...

Yet this little Springtime Blossom
In the confusion of Winter's tricks
Showed the Path to Awesome
Since Her Inner Clock still ticks...

To a different Time and Zone
Where Joy shakes up Convention
And reminds us that in Heaven's Home
God shines through us Invention!

So this Human past her 'Blooming' stage
Followed suit and Danced ...
With Flower till the end of day
Without a Seasoned Glance.

'Twas time to go, for now was cold
As Nature took the moment-
But it couldn't take their sharing bold
And what they learned from growin':

    "No matter what Your 'Season'
    Every One was Born to Dance
    Beyond all Human Reason
    Beyond all Blooms of Chance.

    We are All Expressions-
    Something Greater than our Part
    And That, my friend, is how Begins
    The Art of Who You Are!"

"Rhyme Of Release"

When you've said your Peace,
Yet still Feel needs for Healing All Around...
Give Up your needs to The Higher Lead-
Let Go- Let God Profound.

Let Go Into The Angels Wings
To Gather broken pieces...
And Heal them into Better Things
Till All Uncertain Ceases.

THE Great Healer puts out Feelers
To see the Best Solution.
LOVE'S the Seeker to heal the Meeker
To Give Strength and Resolution.

No One on earth can take your Worth-
In whatever 'Form' it tries.
Compassion sees Past You and Me
To Re-Birth a Dream That Dies.

So, Let Go Into The Angel's Arms...
Release All Pains and Cares!
Let Miracles Transform with Art

Let Go-

Let Kindness Share!

"Shark Sightings"

When Swimming with The Sharks in Life
In waters known for Peace,
Look Up to See Hope's Guiding Light
Still streaming through The Deep.

Call upon The Angel Crew-
Their Promise To Rescue You.
Your Lifeboat's Coming-
Keep Hope's Heart Strings Strumming...

Vibrating You Home To Truth.

"SomeDay"

"Some Day I'll Be Who I'm Meant To Be-
Some Day I'll Share My Soul-
Some Day I'll Live In Total Peace-
Some Day I'll Reach My Goal!"

But "Some" isn't on my calendar-
Just numbers passing by...
"Some" will soon Surrender
To a Time to say 'Goodbye.'

It's Time To Live To Be -To Stream-
New Episodes of 'Now'
Time To Live 'As If' your Dream
Is Already Living 'How.'

It's Time to Let Go Dated 'Oughts'
That held your Real Self down.
Waiting for that 'Dream' you Thought
Would earn your Higher Crown.

The Greatest Irony on Earth
Is the 'Horse before the plough'-
The plough can't move without the Birth
Of a Horse that Lives In 'Now.'

Nothing Moves Without 'The Now'
However slight its budge-
"Some Day" never comes this way-
The Future knows no judge.

So BE Your "SomeDay"-
Be It NOW-
As if Tomorrow never was.
For In Essence, There's Only 'Presence'...
You ARE The Dream You Trust!

"Divine Pottery"

When Someone says...

"That Mold was Broken" or "There'll Never Be Another,"
We Bless the 'Mold' - Unique, now Grown
Into Its Legendary Cover.

Then realize in God's Design,
He Creates more of Its Brothers-
With Different Shapes and Different Size-
Appearing unlike Another.

Yet Being More Alike Than Different,
In This Universe So Bright-
We Find God's Essence and Eternal Expression
Reminding us His Light...

Shines On in New Creations -
Ever Inventing More to Love
In this Ever Expanding Nation
Of God's Expression from Above.

"Leafing Alone"
(Story Of The Leaf That Left)

Said The Breeze to the Leaf
As it fell from the Tree,
"I know you feel lonely
By yourself as you leave...

But know 'Alone'
You never will be-
Because of Who made
The Leaf and the Tree.

I was sent to remind you,
Though 'See' me you can't,
You can Feel My Soft Presence
If your Heart takes a Glance..

Of the Moving Around you-
Because of My Breeze,
You can see the Results
Though unseen in the Trees.

I Am Here To Support you.
Let my Breeze help you Dance
With my Invisible Soul Tunes-
Let us Fly, Take a Chance!

And Land on Another-
You'll be Their Sign
As was Me-
To assure all your Brothers
God Looks After Each Leaf-

Even when They Must Leave..
He Leaves You With Peace.

"Flower Power"

A Beautiful Red Flower
In the middle of a street,
Had no control who passed each hour-
Or how close would come their feet.

Her Color Shone into Each Soul-
Whate'er their steps would cross.
Even when ignored, she Glowed-
Whether they 'Got It'- or not.

A Lesson learned from Little Flower
Leaps Tall as the Tallest Trees:
It Matters not if others cower-
When God's Love Lives Through Your Leaves.

"Flying Human"

A Free Spirit Dancing Joyfully
In The Univers-ity Of Life
Lived her days so playfully
But curious of Human Plight.

And so she asked her Creator
About their Adventure there -
And If Sooner or Later
She could Experience
Some of their Human Cares.

And as Time would manifest
Her Thought to Live that Dream,
She discovered what she'd have to Invest
In Living The Human Scene:

No more Flying Freely
In Pure Bliss Effortlessly-
One had to work for Freedom
By Living Consciously.

No more Only Seeing Goodness -
It's Different Here On Earth:
As Politeness walks with Rudeness
And Sadness walks with Mirth.

So perplexed she was, she had to Meet
With The Creator Of It All
And asked Him, what's The Lesson
In this Contradictory Call?

And with a Gentle Kindness
That Only The Purest Can Be,
He quietly and calmly
Shared His Recipe:

"My Child, in order to Fly in Bliss,
You have to Let Go Of Fear.
In order to turn a Life as This,
You see Opposites as Peers.

Without The Dark, we'd know no Light.
Without the Tears, no Joy.
But the Key is turning On The Light,
For Darkness to avoid.

The Power Of your Freedom
To Fly in Total Bliss,
Is learning how to Live In It
When pain is all there is.

Just as you Think to summon Wings
To Fly Above the clouds,
So must you Think and Feel and Be
To turn a frown around.

We're Spirits here to Heal this world,
To learn to Live Through All.
Remembering where we came from First-
Is The Purpose Of "The Call."

CONNIE FREEMAN PRINCE

"Detours To Enlightenment"

So What Do We Do To Be Enlightened?
When Unexpected Delays
Make a world where we feel frightened-
Where Hope once filled our days...

"Welcome To Your Path Of Growth!"
Said the Unassuming Sage:
"Time ya Learn What Matters Most-
When you're Challenged To Be Brave!"

When This Univers-ity Of Life
Shakes Up your 'Every Day'-
With what Appears to block your Sight-
Remember from Whence You Came.....

You Came Here For A Higher Purpose-
Much Higher than old ways
That Appear to Re-Surface
When approaching Destiny's Play...

"What Do You Do To Be Enlightened?"
Once again replies The Sage:
"You Still Chop Wood, and Carry Water"-
It's ALL Part of God's Play!

The Night Still Turns To Day...
Live LOVE, Live PEACE-
And PRAY

Day By Day
Hour By Hour
Minute By Minute
Second By Second

Time Clocks Wait For No One -
Step By Step
Inch By Inch
Live In The Now:
There Lives Life's 'How.'

"For the Uncertain Traveler"

Remember.....
The Witch's Forest will oft Appear
On Your Way To Oz-
Ignore the 'Flying Monkeys'
Keep Faith with All You've Got!

The Emerald City Inside Your Soul
Depends on Where You Look
Your Yellow Brick Road will help you Grow
On The Path The Angels took:

They Co-Author Your Life's Book!

"Looking Out Your Inner Window"

Did you Notice -- the Green of Trees was there in your deepest pain?
Did you Notice -- the Beauty of the Sun, Shining through the rain?
Did you Notice -- the Shade by that Tree was created by the Sun?
The Dark and Light -- The Day and Night, is just how Life is Run.

We can step into the Darkness -- We can Step Outside the Rain --
The Choice is ours, depending How, and Where we put our pain.
We can let it run its Nature's Course, diffusing it in Light,
As Shadows disappear exposed and Faced -- there is no fright.
Resist it not, the Sun so hot -- it cools in time with rain.
And,
Did you Notice -- the Green of Trees was there in your deepest pain?

189

"God's Favor"

A little Tulip Flower,
In the Shade of A Mighty Oak,
OverPowered by branches showered -
Still, In Its Sun, she woke...

She asked their Great Creator,
Who Created Both of Them,
Which of them were Favored-
For all She had was stems.

That Big Oak Tree seemed So Strong-
Overpowering all we see-
But what she didn't realize was
The Beauty She Could Be!

Simply Being Full with Color
Rich and Deep in Hues-
When it came to pick a Flower,
She's the One That Humans choose.

Now the Oak, All Folk Sure Loved-
And basked within Its shade-
Both Oak and Flower displayed Each Hour
Expressions God had made.

In the scheme of Earthly things
Remember, None Shines Better-
Each of God's Expressions Sing-
Each Represents a Letter...

In the Alphabet of Life
Each Different for a Reason
We're All Expressions:
Joy or Strife--
There's a Beauty in All Seasons.

So never worry or try to hurry
Or Strive to Be the Tree.
For in Heaven, there is no jury-
Just Be What You Can Be...

Every Flower, Every Tree-
Elephants and Ants,
Have More Importance than we see-
They're All Part of The Dance!

Each was given Their Own Mission,
One No Greater Than The Other-
When measured by The Holy Vision:
We're Offspring from God's Mother-
Connected: We're All Brothers!

"Death by Expectation"

Does God expect a Willow Tree
To Grow Apples in the Spring?
Or expect a tiny Bumble Bee
To Grow an Eagle's Wing?

Then why do We expect
Those who cannot See,
To be aware and show more care
When they see through just their 'me'?

So let The Willow Be a Willow
And Let The Bee just Be.
Expect Nothing - Or die in suffering
Expecting Others See-
Through the Limits of their 'Me'.

Judge Not, and Let It Be.

"God's Son Screen"

When The Hot Sun's Blazin' In this world-
And you're Feelin' Fried,
Put on your 'Spiritual Sunblock'
To protect what you can't hide.

For the 'Humanly Fair' Complected,
Pale by Comparison,
Put on your 'Spiritual Sunblock'
And you're baking will be done.

It's a scary world when tempers hurl
Up to a Hundred Degrees!
So put on your 'Spiritual Sunblock'
And put your Soul at Ease.

Your SPF Of Peace.

"After Thoughts"

I asked for Patience
I asked for Strength
I asked for Forgiveness
Then God sent a 'Link'...

To Download Within
What His Wisdom would send
More Lessons Begin
When we Choose to Transcend:

Something from which to be Patient About-
And Something I Must Forgive-
Someone I Must Be Strong Around-
He Sent Me Reason to Live.

Every Thought is a Lesson-
Manifesting in Time...
Be Careful What You Ask For-
You WILL Get a Sign.

Above All, Be Kind
In Training for The Divine.

If you've ever felt like saying:
"Stop the World, I wanna get off!"
This Poem's for You:

"On Your Axis"

Ever Evolving Ever Changing
Ever Spinning Round-
This ole world is a 'Trip' for many...
Keeping Feet Upon The Ground.

Upside Down, yet Up We Stand
In this Univers-ity Of Life.
God's Gravity keeps us on land
As Day spills into night.

It challenges Perspective -
Depending where you stand.
Your Soul remains your Key Detective
In a tiny grain of sand.

Set your Sights on the Massive Ocean-
And risk your feelings drown.
Or on The Mountain Top, Devotion
To the Flying Eagles' Rounds.

It all depends from whence you View
Your Journey passing through-
That 'Still Small Voice' Inside Of You
Still Knows Your Path To Truth.

Breathe High
Breathe Deep
Breathe New.

195

"For the Unassuming"

A Daisy on a Highway
Saw a Billboard on its road:
Advertising Flowers:
"Next Exit, Beauty Flows!"

Many cars passed by her-
Not knowing she was there.
She had no fancy fodder-
Just what Nature made her wear.

She'd often feel unnoticed,
No 'Billboard' of her own.
Feeling in her solace,
Disrespected where she'd grown.

And then one day a car broke down
And a saddened family sat.
Waiting for a ride to town,
Sad what Fate had cast.

Then a little girl ran up to her
And picked this Daisy's stem.
And found her Bright Color stirred
An unexpected grin...

That in this unassuming place
God planted Spirit food.
To remind when others know no trace-
Their Purpose Lives for Good.

So next time you feel unnoticed
By the ego world's 'Billboards,'
Remember that God's Focus
Is on Heavenly Rewards.

"Spirit Strength Training"

And The Dragon Growled:

"Why are you Surprised I'm Here?
Remember The Hero's Tale?
On the way to Stars, There's Fear…
The threat that you may fail.

Flying Monkeys could take sail-
Flying by your window....
Challenging your Sight and Flight-
Putting Dreams in Limbo.

It's just a puzzle piece you'll find
On Your 'Road to Right.'
Face Them with The Courage
Of Your Little Child So Bright!

Strength not always comes from 'Tough'-
Sometimes 'Strong' must bend-
Into The Shape Of Gentle Power
That needs Love's Light to Send...

As even Dragons need a Shower
To calm them down with Love.
Face them, Trace them, Watch them Race when
You Think they feel Too Tough.

And watch The Power Of Love embrace them-
Love Leaps Past All Lengths...
Hold your Head High-
Let no disgrace in.
Great Love Empowers Strength!

That's How Greatness Thinks.

"Living Big"

An Anonymous Earth Angel
Retired to the Pearly Gates,
And as she tried all angles,
She wasn't sure she Lived her Fate.

St. Peter asked, "What concerns, my child?
You seem concerned you came."
And humbly she replied a cry,
Distinct to Human Aims.

Many asked if I "Made It Big?"
In earthly measures seen,
And I had no answers but "I Tried"-
Though felt More that I could Be.

St. Peter turned and looked at her
With Gentle Knowing Eyes,
And with Eternal Wisdom Sure,
In his Kindest Tone, replied:

"What is "Big" In earthly terms
Can be taken in due Time-
But what is "Big" In Heaven,
Never dims Its Shine...

Were you Kind?
And Were you Caring?
And Loving to All Mankind?
"To the least of these, my Brethren"
Is How the Highest measure Time.

Ego gains will come and go,
As Fame will- all will find.
But what Lasts from every Past:
Did you Live Life Kind?

For if you did, You've helped a Life
See the Love God Sees-
Which will surpass rewarded tasks
A Human Judge believes.

If you've touched a Hurting Heart,
You've made a Heavenly Start-
The Highest Purpose Star of Stars-
Are The Highest Form of Art.

If you've Lived The Love you Give-
From That Place of Grace God Is,
My Child, In Truth, your Star's not missed-
You've Made It - "Made It Big."

Loving "Big's" What Heaven IS-
The Biggest "Making It Big!"

CONNIE FREEMAN PRINCE

"News at Eleven"

(A Call Up to Heaven)

Where is the 'Kind' in HumanKind?
Where did it go? Where can we find
A Country of Conscience Of Kind Like Minds
No matter the Race, we Run with Time...

Have Mercy upon the ill of mind
Let them Not Control us
Let Wisdom Again our Sanity find
Make our Home a place to Trust.

But first it Begins With the Kindness we lend -
Kindness we've seen lack.
We miss you So, our Faith Filled Friend
"Do Unto Others" Come Back!

(A Poem Inspired by my Sweetheart
On A Cherished Day Upon Our Hill Top)

"News Worthiness"

For Every One Bad Thing-
A Million "Loves" are Said
For All Reports Newscasters Ring
Live Stories that are Glad

For All Sad News of Deaths and Illness
There are More Alive Today-
Living On In Wellness
And On at Heaven's Gate

So next time the News is Overwhelming
And 'Bad News' brings you Pain
Remember LOVE is Still Revealing
GOODNESS Still Remains!!

"Speaking Your Truth"

So you have Something to say to Someone
To Finally 'Speak You Truth'
You have Something from whence begun
This Path you have pursued.

But The Catch becomes a Truth Unsung-
If captured, could undo
The Loving Peace that you have won
Pursuing Higher Views.

Do you tell this Piece of Hell
That's Haunted Dreams pursued...
Or Pray for Peace, Forgiveness swell
And let your Soul Live Truth.

Do you wanta be Right or Happy?
The Choice is Up To You.
Ether Let Go- or Let it Grow
Into ugliness rebuked.
Ask God: Please Help!
His Power's Inside You!
Peace: The Ultimate Truth.

"Speaking UP"

Whenever it Feels Uncomfortable
To Speak Your Truth and Breathe,
Remember-
Your Soul's Unstoppable
Your Truth Will Set You FREE!

Whenever a Confrontation
Shakes you to your core,
Remember there's Liberation
Being What You're Put Here For.

Speak From Your Heart
Speak From Your Soul
Speak From Your Deepest Parts.
But Most Of All, Speak LOVE you Know:

The Voice Of Who You Are.

"Our lives begin to end the day we become silent about things that matter." -- Martin Luther King Jr.

"Political Correctness"

When 'Political Correctness'
Slams Freedom of Speech
And downs Directness
An Artist perceives ...
Does 'appropriate'
mean you cannot say
What's in your Heart,
Seen another way?

What makes our Country 'Great' it seems
Is not just policy planned to be -
It's the Freedom of each Woman and Man
To Live their Truth, with varied stands.

And to those who claim their 'Christian' roots,
Is this Truly 'What Jesus Would Do?'
Say hurtful things to one another
Cause they disagree, so hurt their brother?

Have Mercy on our Country, God,
Not just for what it stands for -
But for its people who have forgot
That Grace is what we came for.

"Poetic Justice"

This is for the Critics-
Who judge with words as swords-
Whose Harsh thoughts forgot Who taught
We Come from The Same Source.

The saddest part for Any One
Who speaks without a Heart-
Is the fact your judgment soon will run
Into The Soul Of Who You Are.

And There's Where Karma Starts.
Beware As Words Depart....
For What You Say -- You Are.

205

"Power Lifting"

Be Strong in your Gentleness-
Be Meek in your Strength -
Be Kind in your Courageousness -
Be Careful What You Think.

Life is a Potpourri ...
A Mixture of All Things-
Where Opposites are On Top of It
And CoHabit Winter/Spring.

So Be Strong In Your Gentleness.
For There's The Greatest Strength:
Like Music in Life's Silenceness...
Strong Love is Heaven's Link.

There's Power How You Think.

"Power Protectors"

I Finally Got It:
It Doesn't Matter
If one fails to see your Worth,
Or dis-respects Why You Are Here-
They Have No Power To Hurt.

The Only Power That Runs You,
They cannot touch, for sure.
You Will Rise Above With Truth-
And all the small endure.

So Hold Fast To Who You Are-
Hold Fast, And Hold Your Heart.
Let Them Not Near-
What You Hold Dear-

Blind Souls can't see the Stars.

"A Vote for Peace"

For Peace of Mind
For Human Kind
Bring Back The 'Kind' in Human-
Original Offspring of The Divine,
Help Us Live What We're Pursuin':

A Vote for Faith
A Vote for Care
At Least we have The Choice.
To Vote At All's a Freedom
So Many fought to Voice-
So whatever Choice you make Today,
Let us not forget -
The Power in The Voice that Prays
Is what makes Our Country Best!

"Hope VOTES!"

Enough 'One Voice'
Enough 'One Vote'
Enough Stand Up For Good-
Is What Make Us 'United' States
Freedom Is Understood.

But Each Must Take A Stand For Truth-
Each Must Play Their Note -
In The Symphony Of Free-
Be The Change- And VOTE!

"....And They Rise"

This is for
The Young and The Brave-
The Young At Heart,
Who Stand Up To The Grave.

This is for
The Passionate Ones-
Who Will Change The World
For Their Daughters and Sons.

Take Heed, the Callous,
Whose Intention is Greed-
Whose own Self Interest
Amends to no Need.

For The Future's in Sight
For New Hearts and Souls,
Whose wounds hold Their Rights-
As Our Country Unfolds....

The Land of The Free
Who Speak with Brave Love-
With Democracy-
Time to Vote:
Time Is Up!!

"R-E-S-P-E-C-T"

When someone treats you with Lack Of Respect,
Remember The Source it came.
Mistreating Power is the Ultimate Neglect
Of The Wisdom of The Sane.

It's Subtle how it Can Creep In-
From a simple 'Tone Of Voice'
Or perhaps a Lack Of Listening-
Disregard of Another's Voice.

The Best Recourse is to Be The Light-
Even when One's Darkness Shows
They Cannot Touch The Pure In Sight-
They Cannot Stop Your Growth.

We all come from The Great White Light -
Encompassing Every Shade.
And if you Dis another's Sight,
You Dis What God Has Made.

Help Us Forgive Depraved.

"BE"

BE The Breath That You Breathe In-

BE In This Moment NOW.

BE The Peace you wish Transcends

From every country's crowd.

Life is a Vibration-

You Choose to Focus On.

BE Its Celebration-

And You'll Reach God's Love Beyond....

Inside-

Where It All Comes From.

"One"

Take Away the Language-
The Different ways we share-
Take Away the Colors,
The Different Clothes we wear-

Take Away the Borders,
Upbringing and Belief-
And Underneath it All you'll find
The Truth Of You and Me.

The Source of every woman and man,
The Stardust in our view
Is The Essence where our Souls Began-
The Truth of Me and You.

May we Meet our Likes and Differences
In The Middle Land Above,
And Remember our Cross References
Were Made From God's Same Love.

One Life, One Daughter, One Son.

"One is All"

To our friends on every Island
And All Round The Globe
All Sisters, Brothers - though unknown-
Connected by Our Soul.

When we Pray for One,
We Pray for All-
None separate from The Son.
Angels Answer Every Call
As Open We Become...

For awhile upon this Earth-
The While that we're All here-
Help us God to heal the hurt,
To gently soothe the tears.

Right This Moment-
Right This Time-
Let Each Breath, Exhale Peace
To send Around This World to find
The Ways To Help Hate Cease-

Peace To All
Send Peace

"Out of Reach"

Do you ever Feel You're Missing Out
On Moments others see?
'Timing' you have later found,
You thought you ought to Be?

Did you ever think that maybe
You are Where You're Meant To Be?
Or else you would not be there-
To Each, His Destiny.

Does God put extra Value
On a Lion or Giraffe?
They Each live Truth they're Born Into-
They don't even have to ask.

So next time you feel you're 'missing out,'
That Life has passed you by...
Never measure your Unique Now
By Another's 'Me' or 'I'-

We Each Live Our Own Time.
Live Light. Live Love. Live Kind.
Your Destiny Will Shine.

"Overcoming"

When you know your Heart's Intent's In Tune
With Only Love and Joy,
Let not another hurt your Truth-
For you know Who God employs.

Send Only Love, Always Love-
Replace what smaller see.
Must take The Chance to Rise Above-
For True Creativity.

Breathe Deep - You're Born To Be.

"Seeing In The Dark"

This is for The Lonely Hearts
Those torn apart when Love departs-
This is for The Disillusioned
When Dreams are dimmed in this world's Confusion.

Never Give Up on Hope Eternal!
New Days Still Dawn from Dark Nocturnal.
And as the Darkness falls again,
Hold On to The LIGHT-
Your Angel Friend.

Hold On to The Sight of a Promised Sunrise
Even when seen another demise.

Hold On to The Hope
To How Angels Cope.

Through Holy Eyes,
See Love Survive.
In The Comfort of Angels
Let your Healing Heart Thrive.

"Light in Darkness"

She felt her Light be darkened-
Soul Breath that blew around...
She felt so deep she harkened
The Angels come to ground.

Why? She asked, is there so much Pain
In a world God promised Joy?
Why? How can a world be sane
With unexpected ploys?

Then as Deep as the Breath around That Light
Blew hers to and fro-
She could Feel the Breath of God Flow
Bright Deep Inside her Soul.

And realized she must Breathe His Breath-
She must Feel His Feelings Through-
For her Light to Shine through Life and Death
It can't just come from 'you.'

So she surrendered all her disbelief
Of all this cruel world's ways,
And Offered it Up for Soul Relief
To help live out her days....

For there is No End to the Light God Lights
There is No End Above-
Remember through your Darkest Nights,
God Lights Our Light In LOVE!

"Salve for Your Soul"

When the world feels harsh
And it's hard to start
One More Day With Hope,
Just Remember Who You Are:
God's Child who's Born to Cope.

Hold On To Hope
And ne'er Let Go-
For right around the bend...
Are Miracles assigned to show
Love's Comfort Angels Send.
Hold On- Begin Again
You're Loved, by Heavenly Friends!!

"Peace In the Process"

There's Peace in the Process
With Focus on Pure Love
Peace Begins With Inner Recess
From the ego driven tough.

Focus on The Beauty
Will Manifest More Of
Putting Joy within your duties
Helps your Heart to Rise Above!

"Shh!!

*Are You Sill Looking
For God to send a Sign??"*

All you need is right there Cooking
Just Listen and you'll find:

The 'Every Day' sends More your way
than your Earthly Ear can Hear-

All you Have to Do is Be Aware of What's in Front of You:
Good or Bad, There's Truth Of What or Not To Do.
How's It FEEL?? Does It Feel REAL?
The Truth's Inside Of You!

"Sight...Seeing"

In this Life of Technicolor,
Some See just 'Black & White'
How do you open Hearts to Fuller-
When refused to Open Sight?

That's when you put on 'Spirit Shades'
To protect your Vision's Soul.
Don't Let the Limited degrade
How Color Makes Us Whole.
Keep Following Your Flow...

"Skywriting"

She drew upon the Sky of Mind
    Colors and Words and Songs.
She knew she had to paint for Signs
    To lead where she belonged...

Clouds of different formations
    Danced Inside her Soul-
Looking for Transformation
    In time to reach her Goal.

And since they were free flowing
    There were no frames to fit,
So her images kept growing
    There was no time to sit.

She couldn't pin them down with words
    As they were far too high to write.
So she kept her thoughts free flowing-
    So many out of sight.

High Inside The Sky of Mind
    There are no worldly limits.
Forever There lives all God's Kind:
    The Eternal Land of Spirit!

"It's A Moment!"

Catch it before it goes...
Slipping through the cracks of Time-
Gone before you know.

It's A Moment!
Relish every second
Living Awareness In This Now-
Is The Key of Love that beckons...

When Life is filled with Rushing Around,
Let One Moment Stop In Time-
And Remind us Greatest Joy Is Found
In The Moment-
Peace Abounds

God's Love Is All Around!

As you Inhale This New Day:

"Sweet Breath Of Life"

I'm Breathing In The Breath Of Peace-
So Deep It Fills My Soul...
And Wraps Its Breaths Around All Tests
Of Human Fears I know.

I'm Breathing In The Best Of Thee
To Comfort what feels old-
Reviving what my Soul's been striving-
To Be The Love You Grow.

And as I hear the Sounds Of Life
Reminding I'm Still 'Here,'
I Breathe In The Breath I cannot See-
And Feel Your Presence Near.

I Breathe Relief from Tears.
In You, There Is No Fear.
Sweet Breath of Life-
Sweet Cheer!

"In The Peace of Our Beloved"

My Favorite Word: BELOVED.

My Favorite Feeling: PEACE.

My Favorite Highest Summit

Is Living in Both with Thee.

As Daily Life with all its Stress
Of Constant Upkeep Be
Finds Comfort Best
And Sweet Soul Rest
When through Eyes of LOVE we SEE.

Beloved, Peace pray Be with Thee
Beloved Sweet Peace Be
Help us Breathe Your Love So Deep
To set our Spirits Free!

"Sweet Dreams Prayer"

Sweet Dreams to All, and Let It Be.
The Past is Gone, no longer to see-
Sweet Dreams to All, and Let It Be.
I Thank You for each memory!

Time moves us Now to Greater Days.....
With Healing- Each a Special Date!
Another Chance to Live our Dreams
Another Chance for Spirits Free !

Dream Each Day, Make Each Soul Smile!
I Surrender All, Each Unknown Mile...
I Surrender Dreams and Dare To Be
The Essence of God's Inner Peace.

Here Be.

Sweet Dreams and Breathe!

Deep Breaths, Breathe In

Let Be!

LOVE Each Moment, Each Second we're Growin' ...

Let Live - Love Give-

Sweet Dreams!

"Take A Breath"

Dear Breath of God
Who Breathes Through All
Who Gives Us Life
We Give You Awe.

Expressing through
When we're In Tune
Your Light infused
In Sun, In Moon.

Help Us Connect
Dear Breath of Life
And share Respect
Through Joy, through strife.

For The Only Peace
That Breathes with ease
Is The Love ne'er cease
That Breathes Through Thee.

Dear Breath of Life,
Live You, Live Me.

"I Feel That Train A Comin'..."

Being Still on a Moving Train-
As each window changes scenes...
If you're Really Still you can almost Feel
The Grass beneath your feet.

.

Though this world's in constant motion,
You have The Power to Stop.
Take a Breath- Live Devotion
In This Moment-
Is All You've Got.

Though Fast it seems- It's all a Dream
Changing with the wind...
The Only Constant is What You See:
Choose to See Within-

Where Real Life Begins.

"Thoughts For Kin"

Moments made with Family
Whether Near or Far
Are Moments to be Cherished
For they're part of who you are.

I've often grieved of limited time-
As time in life goes fast-
But try we will to make them fill
With Heart Memories to last.

So as a New Day Breaks Again,
We pray Peace To All We Love.
And that God Bless All our Family and Friends
With Angels from Above.

"Gratitude"

When no words come close to Express -
Your Depth of Gratitude,
Is when you Call On Angel Spirits
To speak your Grateful Truth.
I wish I could return in portion
All you mean to me -
My Oh So Humble Heart Knows Fortune
For All through You I've Seen ...

I Pray that all your Kindness shown
Returns a million fold -
As among All Angels it is known:
God's Gratitude is Gold.
A Gift True Love Beholds.

"This Too Shall Pass"

An Imperfect Song
For All Who've Lost
At Priceless Cost
With Hearts So Tossed.

We Give, We Live, We Be, Belong
Where Love Lives Grateful:
Survives The Strong!

"Soul Call 911"

When a Situation Cuts your Core
With an Attack upon your Peace-
Breathe In Deep and Call Your Lord
To Heal What You Can't See.

Call The Name Of The Holy Christ-
Release the Toxic Grasp
Of those Attacking your Soul's Right
To Live In Peace that Lasts.

Call Upon Your Angels
Call Upon Your God
Call For Help From Every Angle
Replace All Angst With Love.

Within, Without, Above!
Call on The Wings Of Doves.

"Deep 'See' Fishing"

In shark infested waters, Devotion
Keeps her swimming through the Night.

Do you Focus on staying afloat-
A Fish out of Water's Soul-
Or Focus on finding a boat
To take you to your Goal?

When Up Ahead, a Distant Light
Shines Upon the Shadows-
Looking Up, a Glorious Sight
Showing Possible New Meadows...

She Focused on that Brightest Light
Clearing murky shores...
Signs of Care - New Hope she Shares:
Break Free The Ocean's Floor!
Let Light Show You The Door!

"Cloud Casts"

A Cloud flew by Two Searching Souls, Awaiting New Creation.
As It knew How It would be known- Was up to Interpretation.

One saw an Image of an Angel- One saw a Vulture's Wing.
It all depended on the Angle Their Inner Eye would bring.

As One can only See The Sky From the Lens of Their Own Eye.
If what you 'See,' your Soul defies, Then Truth will pass you by...

All Clouds have Neutral Meaning- Just as Day & Night.
Love or Hate is Your Revealing- Of How you View each Sight:
God Help Us See Your Light!
Let Love Reveal What's Right!

229

A Day on A Healing Journey:

"Dandelion Days Have Healing Ways"

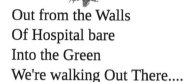

Out from the Walls
Of Hospital bare
Into the Green
We're walking Out There....

In overwhelmed numbness
Of shared Overload
Of feelings we've seen
That's forced us to grow.....

Hand in Hand-
More forms to fill out-
Living Faith through each Prayer
So Real we could shout.

We walked into Sunlight
After Hours cool steel
Free for awhile
Calm Moments to steal.

My Beloved looks down
The sidewalk we're on
To notice One Flower
Making Itself known

The Brightest of Yellow
In a sea of dark green
Its roots in concrete
Looking Way Up to see...

That though it's surrounded
By unnatural land
It somehow managed
To take a bold stand!

To Greet mere humans
As us passing by
With wonder if we were
Trapped too and tied...

To these bodies imperfect:
Our Gifts to Garage
Our Souls on this earth
In this Life, a Mirage.

This little Dandelion
Yelling out in its Yellow
Without even tryin'
Sang silent 'Hellos!'

A Sign! I mused
To my Beloved to use,
Even Nature seeks Truth
When Survival's pursued.

So to you on Your Path
Whether Flower or Human,
May we All find what lasts
As our Time is Illumined

Life gets our Attention
The most surprising of ways
Even the smallest of Nature-
Stretches to Pray!!

"A Very Short Poem for Short Meetings with Short –
or not so Short people or people who may be Short with you."

Every Face you meet each day
Divine Appointments Be
Look Into Their Eyes and Pray
God Show Their You In Me.

"Southern Fried Thoughts"

When The Heat has creeped,
And Too warmly sneaked
Into the crevices of your Brain...
And your legs and liver start to Quiver
And Crackle and Complain-

Take a Leap into the Deep
Conscious of The Sane-
You know The One,
Who made The Sun-
The Son Shine in the Rain.

Take Mental Breaks and Dip Into
The Melting Pot Of Peace.
Visualize The Path to Kind-
Be Kind and Be Released...

Release to Peace-
And Feel The Breeze
Soothing All It Meets.
And When a Thought feels
'Over Done,'
Turn The Burner Down Beneath...
Relax, Renew and BREATHE!

"Star Sightings"

In an Overwhelming World
Of Billions in this Race,
Toward The Finish Line on Earth,
Who Lives Without A Trace?

When feeling Lost amongst the crowd,
Remember Who You Are.
There Is No Measure to God's Sweet Treasure:
Each Part's God's Heart-
One Star.

"Spirit Showers"

The Gentle Rain
Whispered to the Pane
As it fell

On earth's thirsty feet...

Soothing The Pain Of Past harsh terrain
With a Gentle Caress to the street.

With the Cycle Of Sun,
A New Day's Begun
With a Cleansing from Almighty One-

Let the Rains Fall
Clearing Out, Clearing All
Dancing Rain, Making Sane

Angel Call!

"Soul Reboot"

When Overwhelmed by Expectations -
Soul smothered by 'too much,'
Is when you need a Revelation-
You need a Higher Touch:

Connect with Higher Energies
Just waiting your 'Plug In'-
Connect with Inner Synergies
Just waiting to Begin...

Refreshing you with a Greater Love
That transpires Human Limits.
Dare to Live In Love Above-
The Limitless Of Spirit.

Connect With Spirit Visits.

Refresh, Renew and Live It!

"Reboot Reprise"

"But God, there are literally Millions-
I feel so small in this world!"
And He answered:
"There Are Trillions-
But We're ONE- In "The Universe."

Prayer:
    Breathe In Me, Oh Mighty God...
    Breathe In Me Your Heart!
Help me Breathe What You're Made Of-
    Through Me, Be Who You Are.

"Soul Blocks"

If you Love your God with All your Heart-
Yet block a brother's Soul,
If you Claim to do your 'Christian' part-
Yet Unforgiveness rolls...

If you hold the least resentment
Towards Anyone in this world-
You block your Soul's Contentment-
It's You who feels unfurled.

Even Those you know are 'justified'
In feeling hurtful from,
Are also from The God they Tried-
Just Forgot they were His Sons.

Those Distant from Our Father's Grace,
Self Destruct in time.
But we must not let them block The Place
Inside Where God Resides.

Wherever there's a Block in Love,
Compassion and His Ways-
We also block The Essence Of
The Light from which we're made.

So Shine Your Light On Those who Fright
And Stand Up, when you must.
But don't forget, we Too Be Less
When we Treat Without His Trust.

"Steering Inner Seas"

Navigators Through Energy
Is what our True Souls Are-
Steering through the Forestry
Of Life Up To The Stars....

Our Feelings are Indicators-
Our Radar in each turn,
Giving Signs to the Kind
Of Scene which might occur.

The only way to Peaceful Seas
Is Tuning Into Thee-
Our Captain, Source Of All Healing
Who steers our Course To Peace...

Help us BREATHE in Winds So Deep
That hit upon our face-
The Winds Of Change That Through You Came...
To take us to Your Place:

Our Retreat on shaky seas.
We sail to Heaven One Day Be Landing-
When our Mission is Complete.

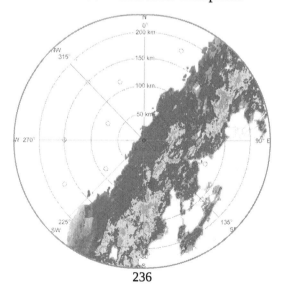

236

"Riding The Rainbow"

She Flew into the mightiest storm
Unguarded Free with Faith.
Counting on her Highest Source
To reveal her Higher Fate...

Yet as The Storm disguised Itself
As simply Nature's song,
Something told her hidden Blessings
Live inside the wrong.

Hold on, Li'l Bird, while flying through
The twists and turns of strife-
For God Promised Us A Rainbow.......

Don't Give Up on Life!

237

"Staying True To You"

Be Authentic-
Not Repentant-
To Who You Truly Are.
When Regulations
Make Alterations,
Don't let them dim your Star.

We're Each Made of Higher Grade,
No Matter what "They" say...
Be True To What You're Born To Do-
And God Will Find A Way!

Prayers Sent UP Each Day

"Do You Hear Her Calling...."
The You you've hidden so long?
She follows you when falling
And lives to be 'on call'

But you have to let her out of there-
Where? Inside of You
She Breathes your Breath
She moves your feet
And Knows your Inner Truth.

Breathe Deeper- Feed Her
No Time Defeats Her
She never gives up The Dream
However long it takes to See Her
Become your 'Inner Me.'

"Return To Sender"

Addressed to my Angels:
(The Filter Through Which
My Soul Becomes Poems)

Your Words Massage the Depths of my Soul-
When My Angels send from Within,
Your Thoughts Make The Depths of me Become Whole.
How Grateful I Am When You Send!

I send you this 'Thank You!'
A note I can't mail,
For Your 'Address' is unknown-
Though I know You prevail...
You're becoming More Real
Each time I get STILL and come 'Home'....'

So I send you this Thank You
Ne'er enough for Your Gift-
In Deep Gratitude,
You're The Reason I Live.

"Divine Appointments"

Every Face you meet each day
Divine Appointments Be
Look Into Their Eyes and Pray
God Show Their You In Me.

"Reality's 'Whether' Report"

It is Raining where we are,
Sunning on other earths.
It is Crying in the Hearts
Who live unspeakable Hurts.

When Tragedy hits Another-
It hits us All in Truth.
For in Essence We're All Sisters and Brothers-
We're All One, Not Two.

So How Can We Help To Ease The Pain,
When Helpless we all feel?
How Can The Sun Shine Through The Rain,
When Another's Hurts Are Real?

Have you ever seen the Sun Breakthrough
An Unexpecting Cloud?
To remind us Light is Still In View
Even when Dark's all around?

Perhaps to work on Our Own Light-
Could help Shine through Life's Doubt...
Perhaps to Shine when none's Around
Could Help Bring Healing Out...

If We're All One, On some Great Level,
To Extend God's Hand of Peace,
Could We Comfort Through The Invisible-
LOVE None Else Can See?

After you've Spoken, Written, and Prayed-
All you Humanly Can-
Perhaps God's Waiting to Work His Ways...
Through The Distant Heart Of Man.

When Will Love Live In Laws Of The Land??

"Recipe Humanity"

Even the Sweetest Recipes,
Most always call for salt-
Sometimes a pinch- sometimes a spoon-
To balance out it all.

The salt brings out the flavor:
The Brightness of the Sweet
Just as the sweetest parts of Life
Are tempered when we meet...

Tears that sprinkle over Joy
That season us with Wisdom
A mixture of the two employ
The Human Heart that Lives 'em.

So whenever Life puts a bad taste
In your mouth, Take Heart.
You're being measured, to make haste
You're a mixture- You're a Part...

Of a Bigger Dish now serving
In The Great Drive Thru of Life
So place your order, you are deserving
Of the sweet & salty slice-

Of Joy & Sadness, Pleasure & Pain
They All make up The Mix
Like Night & Day, & Sun & Rain
This Mystery Dish, God Fix!

CONNIE FREEMAN PRINCE

"Connecting the Nots"

Where Lives the Connection
Between Loved Ones Gone On?
Is it in the Reflection
Of a distant song?

Is it in Remembered Musings
And Boxes and Frames?
What's left can be confusing
Moving on Heaven's to Fame...

What's left can't be filled
With mere Human hands
No matter what's willed
Still Live Greater Lands ...

Where Lives This Connection?
Perhaps Closer to know-
God grant Your Reflection
To see Their New Home.

This Human Frame
Too Soon is Outgrown...
Back where we all came
We reap what we've sown.

Where Lives This Connection?
"In Truth," Sages say,
In Nature's Reflection,
Each Season's New Play."

There is no Death
Continued Is "Essence"-
Re-Cycling our Souls-
Connecting our Presence.

(For Those of 'Joy' moved on...)

"When Laughter Moves to Heaven"

When a Great Laugh is Silenced
In this earthly world,
Heaven's gain's Priceless
Especially with This Girl ~

Will miss you, sweet and funny friend,
But your Memories Remain ....
Can almost hear Relief from Heaven:
"Thank God There's No More Pain!"

Thank You for your Fabulous Spirit!
Thank You for your days!
With Love, we Pray your Soul can Feel it:
Our Gratitude you Came!
Healing Peace we pray you've gained...

"When A Legend Leaves"

When A Legend Leaves Us,
God's Expression also Leaves Us Too.
Which is Why it Profoundly Grieves Us
And Hits our Human Truths.

Some Expressions of The Human Condition
Hit Deep Where God Abides-
Reminding Us Of Life's Transitions...
That never leave our side.

In the Hurried Pace Of Time,
We're Haulted by The Jolt -
Of Stilted Life Who Sends Us Signs:
We're Here To Live Life Bold.
Live Brave.
Live Love.
Live Gold.

"Transcendence!"

From Mourn to Morning
From Day to Night
Life keeps Moving
Revolving Sights
The Gift of Presence:
Unwraps Its Rope-
Re-Birth...Transcendence
New Day! New HOPE!

"Transcendence for Dependants"

How Do we keep One Sick Soul
From ruining Peace In Life?
How Do we keep our Sanity,
With so many crazed in sight?

Now More Than Ever, Light Workers Unite-
And Lift Vibrations So High-
No Shot can pierce Our Vulnerable Side-
No Blow can stop our Flight.

The Unpredictable holds no claim
On Who We Are Inside.
The World can try with pain defame-
But they cannot take our "I."

Our "I AM" is Greater --
Than earthly foe we find.
Our Eternal Souls Know Where To Go-
Hold On, All Human Kind!

God's Grace Still Toes The Line.

Hold On, Transcend These Times.

"When It's Time to Catch Your Breath"

A tiny Breath that used to be
A part of a Hurricane,
Was Short of Breath & felt bereft
Out Powered by its reign...

It seemed that all the Air around her
Was taken by Life's Storms-
As They Bragged of how Their Air would drown her
Into a greater morn.

She knew she had a Purpose-
Though falling short of Breath.
And had to find what hers is
To pass this scary test.

So she Breathed the Air Around her-
The only Hope she had.
And prayed For Miracles Occur
When lack of Breath felt sad.

She Breathed so Deep Within her-
She soon found brand new worlds...
That rose up Well to lend her
The Strength of a long lost girl.

For that long lost girl Inside her
Was starving for Fresh Air
And knew that Truth would endure
All doubt that Hot Air shared.

And Soon she cared no longer
If that Hot Air Hurricane
Tried to steal the Soul of her
For you can't steal God away!

Hope Breathed So Hard It exhaled
All the doubt she harbored there,
She Breathed so Deep her Spirits sailed
Above her Human Cares...

Far Above the Ego Land
That could not understand -
As they could only see
Through sight of man
Too self absorbed in "me's"

So she kept her Sights Above the clan
Forgiving All their Path.
For who knows from where each man may stand
Perception's clouded wrath.

She sailed above the Hurricane
Until Her Path came clear:
To Live in Peace, you First must See

PURE LOVE OUT POWERS FEAR!

"For Our Friends Who've Lost"

What to say when Words cannot
Express Enough when Time's get Tough?

When Loss hits Home for those you care,
We're more than Close -Caught Unaware.

We Pray for Angels when we cannot
Comfort Enough with hurt so rough.
We Pray for Peace when Letting Go
Into God's Hands -
What we can't control.

We Connect With You
One Heart We Show.

"For The Fearful"

Prayers So Deep for those who weep-
Who've lost One Close To Heart.
When nothing left to do or see-
No control from where you are.

We Call Upon The Angels
To rescue what we can't.
We Pray to every angle
To reach to every land.

Please Dear God Please Hear Us...
To Have Faith when lost our Trust.
Please Dear God Be Near Us...
Relieve this Fear unjust.

Prayers So Deep for those who weep-
Help Us Surrender Up
What we cannot do or see-
Help Us Trust Your Love.

248

"For The Haunted"

If some Unspoken Injustice
Still Deeply Haunts your Heart,
Dig Deep – Time to remove it
It's Time for a New Start.

Its poison can taint
What Memories are-
Coming Up to remind you
Unforgiveness is stark.

Surrender It Up
To The Cleanser Of All...
Lay Up at His Feet
Every ounce you recall.

Let Him Transform
All wrongs into right-
By Forgiving the Ignorance
Of Another's cruel plight.

"Father Forgive Them,
They Know Not What They Do"-
The Ultimate Portrayal:
He taught Healing Truth.

Stand Up to Injustice
By Removing its Sting-
Send It To God,
See Miracles Bring!

"For The Forgotten Ones"

If you know the Feel of Dis-Respect,
Hurting worse from "Friendly Fire,"
Let Go their Hold of 'Who You Are'-
They know not your Aims are Higher.

Don't let them take away Your Power-
As you Pray Higher Every Hour.
You're Meant for More - even when ignored.
Don't Let Your Being Cower.

RISE UP!
RISE UP!

Don't Lose Your Trust
In The Power That Brought You Here-

Hold On!
Move On!

Rise from The Dust-
You're Destiny's Still Clear.

BE Here. BE You.
Flee Fear.

"For the Powerless"

When disappointing news
Pierces deep your Heart,
It's easy to assume
The worst for where you are.

But that is when you Have to Pray-
And give up All Control.
And know that NO ONE has the say
To Stop your Destined Goal.

If Ordained by Higher Hands,
No lower powers reign.
Their deeds can't stop Where You'll Land-
When You know from Whence You Came.

Bless and Pray for them All-
And Pray for Good Be Seen.
For with God's Promise, you will not fall-
For HE holds Your Destiny!

"For The Questioning"

When you don't have an Answer What To Do-
Or you Fear The One You're Given,
That's when you call on Angels Tall
To Help The Path You're Livin.'

When you're Frozen in your Inner Tracks
And The Outer are feeling Timid,
That's when you Call for Miracles Tall:
God Strength to keep on Livin.'

Don't let the Unknown hold you down-
Or the Unknowing dim your Light.
Communicate God's Love you've Found,
And Success Will Fill Your Sight-

Hang Tough- No need for Fight.
Grace turns Wrongs To Right.
Love's Light Will Guide The Night.

"AWWKWARD!!"

Why we get embarrassed
Is embarrassing to me.
Cause Every Body's Human-
At least Souls as We Who Breathe.
If Every Awkward Situation
We each have had at times,
Then why pretend we're no relation
To humiliating lives.
May we learn to 'Reelax'
When Life throws us 'Faux Pas'
Cause 'By The Grace Of God' we Last
Past mistakes that cost.
Judge Not- The Best Get Lost.

"For The Whimsical Invisible"

In The Deep Wild World
Of Hopping Humans
Swimming in Energy-
Lived a Soul whose Spirit Swirled
In Invisiblity...

She jumped Up- Then was engulfed
By Bigger Fish Who Flew-
Though She was Made of Highest Grade,
They somehow missed her Truth.

Until She Got - It Mattered Not
Short Sightedness of Others.
When your Mission comes from God,
Your World Is Blessed With Wonders!

It Matters Not The Numbers.
Thus, The Beat of Different Drummers.

"God's Greatest Gift"

For-Giveness Gives For Healing's Help
What Angels Live For Heaven's Health.
Give For Peace - The Greatest Wealth
Transforming Humans out of Hell.

Forgiveness Is God's Greatest Gift
Transforming Hate where Mercy Lives.
We All Are One-
And Need His Peace
By Seeing Him In The Least of These.
Through His Grace, our Souls Find Peace.

253

"The Price of Inner Peace"

When Life has picked and shaken you up
To a Point of No Return...
Remember the Point Returned To
Must be a Point that's Earned....

You Earn your Keep to Inner Peace
By first Giving Up your Hurts -
Giving them Up to a Higher Seat
Where Perspective can occur.

Looking Up Higher Takes More Muscle-
It Takes a Tilt of Your Head~
To Loosen Up the Stiff in us
Takes Breath to Raise the Dead!

But sometimes Life Has to Shake Us Up
To Wake Us Up to see...
As Fire flames to shape Pure Gold,
Let Pain have its way with me...

Let it Flow..... to Purify
By Letting Go the reins
That held it back- twas there attack-
Hurt worse resisting pain.

Let it Flow - Let it Go
Just as the Song so says:
Just Breathe in - Breathe out and Grow
And Let it Be- Just As.

ForGive....Give For
For Giving Gives
Let Be who hurt your soul.
They Give a Gift of Pure Soul Growth
For Giving Makes Us Whole.

ForGiving? For...Giving?
So hard Real Living...
Even when you KNOW you're 'Right!?'
So the ego loves to cry inside
And put up a righteous fight!

You have the choice to kill your Joy
By Giving your Power Away...
We Give it Away as a broken toy:
Takes two to play this game.

As what you Give comes back to you
Your Choice: resent or flee~
Giving Up this fight, this Flight of Fright
Is the Price of Inner Peace!

"Going Down Stream"

It was a beautiful stream-
Except for Just One Thing-
One Thing - One Haunting leaf
An Obstruction to its Peace...

Unassuming passers by-
Or Were They?
Time Will Tell:
If Everything has Its Higher Purpose-
What do Obstructions sell?

What of Obstructions to our Peace?
How do we clear what's there?
When popping up, it's still unleashed....
Don't tell me you don't Care!

Grab it Up and Throw It Out!
Down the River's Tide....
To another fork in The River's
court
To another passerby:

"What of Obstructions to Our Peace?
What of this Haunting Leaf?
If put there out of purpose,
Then like this Leaf- I'll Leave!!"

"Going with The Flow"
Is Highly over rated -
That is, unless You Are That Leaf
And your Destiny feels fated.

Thrown around from whim to worry
By unassuming passers by-
Until one day you Stop the hurry
Of the stream and Dare to Fly....

Above these parts that didn't rhyme
And Just Now changed its course -
This is how you Change Your Time:
Plunge Deeper, Higher Source!

"A Matter of Dreams"
(Soul Truths for The Disillusioned)

Does It Matter
If Dreams don't work out the way your Heart had planned?

Does It Matter
If What You Thought Was Yours was given to another man?

If Asked your Divine Creator Who brought you here to Be....
I wonder what His Angels would answer oh so Tenderly:

"When All the Masters came to share their Higher Purpose here,
Pure Their Intent, yet did not get The Response They held so dear...

When Mankind wouldn't listen, but buried them instead,
They had to Look Still Higher for Where They had been led.

Though Appearances would tell you the Ego World had won,
Remember Daylight always follows The Darkest Moon with Son.

His Bright Light cannot be dimmed- no matter how hard they try.

A temporary shadow cloud cannot kill The Light.
God will find a way to say "Well Done, My Child, Keep High!"
For What Really Matters in the end,
Is That YOU Became The Light!"

"Adrift"

She was drifting on a huge Grand Ocean
That had been on earth for years
She should have felt content devotion
Since many swam through fears...

Yet the waves crashed rough upon her boat-
They rocked her world to test
Which direction? Should she dive or float?
She knew not how to guess...

She could jump and risk her life to Fly
Above the crashing waves,
Or stay the course- Dare to try-
Ignore souls rants and raves.

And then we have the Life Preservers-
A back up plan to death.
But who could say if they deserve her
When all they catch is Breath .....

So keeping head above the water,
Breathe is all she did.
Struggling with all the fish who fought her
And the way she prayed to Live.

So she drifted through the crashing waves
When her compass lost her Dream.
And she Trusted Something Higher Save
The way her life should seem.

When you lose your strength to paddle
You must give up your oars
To The Source that never rattles
And waits for you to Soar ...

So ... Here They Are, My Captain,
Forgive my drifting wings.
Upon Your Waters I cast them
Let my voice Be Yours to Sing!

"As The Thought Turns"

Whene'er you let a Negative Thought
Direct Decisions made,
A Darkness comes Inside your Heart -
And hidden there, it stays…

It colors your Perception
With shades of Soul Untruths-
With unknown Receptions,
That Block The Love In You.

So Whene'er you feel a twinge uncertain-
Uncomfortable energies-
However slight, Take Heed
Take Flight
To Higher Ways To See...

Release to The Great Purifier-
Release to Cleanse your Soul -
And Let God's Peace Heal All You See
And Make Your Spirit Whole.

"Another Dawn"

In the Deepest Silence,
While the World is Spinning Still-
Is a Knowing Presence
Of What Is Really Real.

Though the World is Spinning...
Breathe Still-
In These New Beginnings!
A New Day is ForGiving-
A New Way Is for Living.

In The Deepest Silence,
Breathe Deeply In The Still.
Inside God's Resilience,
Reminds Us He Is Real.

Breathe Deep-
And Dare to Feel.

260

....and then came The News

"To a Speechless Sequel"

I tried to write a Prayer to You
Yet This Time, words are sparse
In a world where Tragedy Renews
And Strikes right through your Heart.

Dear God, we Pray for Guidance,
As we've never prayed before-
Let not more shots ring silence
To Moral Laws ignored.

Guide our Leaders Action Take
Guide Us What To Do-
Let not Insanity re-make
New Normal's horror view.

How to deal with Heartless Souls
Lost in their own hell?
How to comfort Innocence
When No Words make it Well.

May The Miracle of Enough Great Souls
Who Out Number those so lost,
Take back our Country's Conscience sold
With the Price of Human Cost.

Keep Hope! Keep Heart! Keep On!!"

A Prayer - Hurting Times"

Angels Working Overtime,
We Call Upon Your Wings
To Wrap Around all Hearts Entwined
With Unimaginable Grief.

We Pray for Spiritual Guidance-
When News That Strikes Our Souls-
Yearns For Human Kindness,
Comfort Hearts In Hope.

Heaven's Still Our Home.
Send Us Peace To Grow...
Send LOVE To All We Know.

"Re-Runs
For Broken Sons"

Have you ever had bad Memories
Come back to haunt your Heart...
Swept under the rug of sensories
From the Inner Child you are?

Unspeakable the buried pain
No one ever knew-
Secrets that could drive insane
The Innocent in You?

Thus is the life of a Child abused-
Protecting the Ones they Love-
The paradox of feeling used-
Praying for Help Above.

The Ultimate Forgiveness
Is the kind when you're Alone.
For the Price of revealing's Too High for the dealings
Of Pain the seeds then sewn.

So you Face It with your Head Held High
Knowing their seeds of sin,
God in His Mercy will not let by-
Just Give It ALL to Him.

Father Forgive what others don't know
Dealt Dis-Respect to you.
Thus are the Seeds that Ignorance sows
In one's unassuming youth.

Cleanse my Soul of thoughts unjust-
They Know Not What They Do.
And if I stir, I just feel more hurt-
When denied what's known is True.

Help me Let Go, God-
Though it's hard to Forget:
Help me Remember in a Different Way:
Help me Let Go, God
Help heal my regrets
Help heal me as I Pray.

And as I do, I See Through You-
The Greatest Growth Revised:
No good is hurt returned another-
Two wrongs don't make a Right.

So Whatever feels too hard to bare,
It's Time to Change the Past...
By Giving Up to The Highest Care-
Your Deepest Burdens Cast.
Forgive -
For Peace that Lasts.
It Takes A Holy Task.
For Help On High-
Just Ask.
Peace Begins-
When To God You Cast
All Pain - To Heal your Past.
For Peace, Reach Higher-
Just Ask.
Let Go
Let God
Just Ask.

263

"Prayer for Harm's Way"

Prayers for Protection
For All In Direction
Of Uncontrollable Storms...
Our Thoughts and Hearts
Surrounding Compassion...
God Keep You In Angels' Arms!
Pray Calm,
All Winds of Harm.

"A Prayer for the Aftermath"

Pour upon us soaking rain
To cleanse each breath we take-
Pour upon us relief from pain
From this nightmare, help us wake-

To see the One Thing that Still Remains
What e'er life throws our way,
Is more than clothes upon our backs
And things that do not stay...

No flame can tarnish the Human Spirit
However hard it tries!
All Storms Do Pass
Even as we fear it
And The Sun Will Always Rise!

So pour upon our Healing Hearts
The Comfort of all who Care
And from the ashes,
We'll Rise Again
Even Stronger from Love we Share!

Thank You All for Being There!
You Are God's Hands in Prayer.

"Storm Sailing"

There's a raft out in this Ocean
We grasp onto for dear life
While waves of drowned emotion
Overwhelm our sight.

We can struggle with each current
And Try to swim against-
But how can we endure it
When our energy's been spent?

Then as the wind begins to bend
Direction of the waves
What choice have we but to Begin
Again this Life to Save.

Stop struggling with the current
Didn't God make 'current' too?
Stop struggling to endure it
Go With The Flow and Cruise...

Give Up the helm when there is no helm
As you're hanging on for life -
And Trust Our Mighty Captain well
To help the waves subside.

The Most Powerful Control
Is No Control for fight -
How can we know just where To go
When fighting unknown tides?

Float Above the torment
When your arms too tired to fight-
Float Above and Find The Love
Lit from The Other Side.

Keep your eye upon The Lighthouse
The Light will Guide you Home -
The Light Within your Angels send
Your Lifeboat's Not Alone.

"The Waiting Room"

A Sober Sight-
Full left   --   to right-
Those 'On the Mend':
The Fight-

To Heal, To Be, To Get Relief
Each looking for some Light.

All Looks and ages and different stages
Of Similar Dis-Ease.
Backgrounds vary-
But each Soul carries
A Prescription Pad To Peace.

"Take Two of These
If you please
And Call Him In The Morning"...
-Patience, Patient
-Strength to Stay In
This Human Race we're running.

Waiting in The Waiting Room
With Those whose Healing Pray,
Reminds Compassion is The Food
To Nourish Hope Today.

Send Light All Comes Your Way.

"While Waiting In The Waiting Room"

The rumble of the atmosphere
While waiting for 'Results'-
The tumble of the feelings
That fill my soul so full...

It's just the mechanics of 'Earth Machines'-
From The Peaceful to The Frantic.
It's just the process of Human Dreams
And Nature's aging antics..

Waiting and Wondering ... How many years
Are spent in the thundering of clouds passing near...
And pass they all do -Even for You
Waiting and Wondering as Fate reveals Truth

So Rumble and Tumble we go with the Flow
What choice do we have? Where else can we go?
It's called Life on Earth - Within Human Form
It's called Giving Birth To a Brighter New Morn!

Waiting In The Waiting Room
Like a 'Purgatory' be....
Just Whistle a Tune- You'll Find Out Soon-
Whatever Happens, You'll Find Peace.

"Divine Defines"

Let No One Define You-
But The God Who Brought You Here.
Let No One Refine You-
But Your Breath of Life So Dear.

For No Thing, No One-
No Wing, No Sun-
Has Power Over You-

None Shines Brighter...
You Are God's Lighter
To Shine On Earth His Truth

So Shine On past all 'Definers'-
Shine On when 'They' don't know
That No One Knows You Finer-
Than The One Who Made You Glow!

"Hold On!"

Hold Onto Your Truth-
Whatever The View-
Appearing Life's Passed You By...
God Made Each Son
Since Life's Begun
To Be, To Rise, To Shine.

Hold Onto Your Dream
However It Seems
Held back when you don't know why
Trust Up Above
To Deliver With Love
Bless All
Rise Tall
Fly High

Lift Up
Faith Transcends Time
Just BE The Light
And SHINE!

"Breath Nap"

A Breath in the wind
A Pause from fast forward
A Stop Sign in the road
All Three remind us- amidst all the rush
There's Peace turning fast into slow...

Slow...easy does it, say The Breaths that we take
Breathe Deep into Stillness to Grow
Into Sweet Peace and there you'll Awake
To The Place where you're meant to go.

"So much to Do!" Cries the Life around you!
How can you take time to Breathe??
"Cause if you do not," sighed The Soul you forgot,
"You'll forget the Meaning of 'WE!'

For the Breath of Sweet Life Is The Day and The Night
It IS The Sweet Place we can fall
No need to control the Time and The Sight
Just BREATHE, and Peace Will Be All!

"Breathing Peace"

The Peace That Comes from Breathing
Love Deep Within Your Soul,
Only Comes When Seeing
Love Lives Deep In Each We Know.

The Source From Whom All Flows....
Connect and Let Love Glow!

269

"Become The Love"

Become The Love You Wish To Have
Become the Peace You Want To Last
No Obstacle is meant to stay
When You Yourself Were In The Way....

The Way to Peace:
Breathe In Release
Release All Blame-
Let Dis-ease cease.

Release the Pain of what others see
The Way to Sane:
Is To
Let It
Be.

Change Your Lens:
Let Love Perceive
And Become The Love
You Wish To Be.

"Little Divine Appointments"

Life's Little 'Divine Appointments'
Surprise us Every Day.
There's never a Disappointment
When an Angel comes your way!

"Catching Sacred Breath"

In the Deepest Place in our Hearts and Souls
Lives The Connecting Sacred Breath
Breathe Deep Within your Center Core
Breathe Deep Into Its Depths.

The Sacred Lives Inside Us
Though out we grasp for aid
His Comfort waits to Guide Us
But Connection must be made.

What is Inspiration?
Vibrant Faith Breathed In
A Peace-filled Celebration
Increased by what we Send...

Send His Light with each Exhale
Share Forward what you've felt
And Your Search for Peace will never fail
When in The Breath of God You're Held.

"Birth Breaths"

She Breathed The Light
Deep In her Soul
So Deep Within, She'd go...
Its Source not seen, Where Could It Be?
A Glow just God could know.

Not the Glow from the outside Sun
Or even shining Moon.
It came from Where All Life's Begun
The Source of Higher Truth.

She Breathed this Light that filled her Heart
So Bright it beat so Free
And expanded what appeared her part
Into a Greater Lead.

She knew then It needed her
To Materialize on earth.
What good is Light if out of Sight --
So that's why there is Birth!

"Circumstantial Evidence"

"What Evidence Do You Have?"
Asked The Scientist to The Sage.
"Where Is this 'Place' Of Heavenly Grace
On The Universal Stage?

Where Is your Proof Of Divine Existence?
No recorded Birth we see-
Only 'Stories' of Heavenly Glory-
No Real Records left to read."

The Unassuming Prophet
Then looked deep into their eyes,
And responded to this Impossible Quest
Of God in Human Disguise:

"Recorded Proof Of Human Roofs
Can be gone in a Hurricane's Eye.
Does this mean They had never lived,
When no Certificate to find?

When birds Fly by in Beautiful Sight-
Only to be 'lost' in flight,
Does this mean They were Never seen-
Cause they never caught Your eye?

No Proof left of a Beautiful Rose
Whose memory lives in Hearts.
Though stems moved on, with weather gone-
No 'Proof' it lived for Art.

The Miracle Of Birth Itself:
The Only Innocent Time-
When even those of "Evil" throws
Echo The Divine.

Before the world gets hold of them,
Their Purity is True.
Till they forget Who they beget:
The Connection 'tween Me and You.

But perhaps the Greatest Human Proof
Of Steps walked Once Divine,
Is The Miracle Of LOVE let loose-
So Deep It Outlived Time.

Its Power Transforms Nations Lost,
Its Energy so sought-
Who's to say it Manifested
In The Form Of Human Cost?

The Evidence Of Anything
Is in the Song it sighs....
How can Light be Touched in Night?
Its Presence Transcends Sight."

"Embracing Life is Accepting"

Its Mixture of Night and Day...

Light and Dark,
Joy and Pain-

Mankind and All His Ways.

What We Choose To Focus On....

Always Makes The Difference:

The Night's A Sign

Day's Just Behind-

Hold On To Life - God's Present.

"Flying Lesson"

Darkness gives Starlight a backdrop thru which to Shine ...
Your Attitude sets the Altitude for how High your Spirit can Fly!

"Friendly Fire

The most painful blow to one's own soul
Is always Friendly Fire
From one's own camp you've slayed and toiled
To see your Trust expired.

My Heart's been broken by many in life,
But none has hurt the worst
Than where you've shown your Brightest Light
For those you had put first.

When someone shows you lack of Respect,
Remember, Ignorance is Why.
Father Forgive Their Arrogance.
They know not your Heart has Sight.

Take The High Road-
Rise Your Sight!
Don't let them lower your Light.
They Care Not- so Don't Give In.
Shine Anyway- Live Right!
Shine Anyway- Love Bright!

"Help! Is an Appropriate Prayer:"

Help! Heal Me God Out There-
But First Begin where my Soul Is.
Help Me Trust Inside You Care.

Help! Help me Let Go pain,
When others threaten my Sane.
Help me Heal to See The Real-
The Real Purpose That I Came.

Heal Me God I Pray!
Be The Director of my Play.

"Good Grief?"

Why Do We Mourn?
Asked Angel, the Closest One to God,
When we know Our Souls Will Soar
To Heavenly Bliss Above?

Why Do We Cry?
Human Fear Uproars-
When You've Got Our Backs -
You've Got Our Core!

Why can't we Fly?
This Earth Ignores.
Where is Your Guide?
We Pray for More!

Then God Smiled in Sympathy,
As Only He Can Do,
And with His Caring Empathy
Spoke Eternal Truth:

My Child, The Measure of Your Love
Flows in grieving tears...
What's missed is More - than man's made of-
What's missed is Really Near...

Your Loved One's Nearer than what's missed-
The Physical- the Hugs.
Nearer than you Think What Is
Nearer than a Touch...

You Mourn for what was Part of 'ME'-
The Life I Breathed In Him...
You Mourn so Deep it's hard to See
New Life Begins Again...

Know in Every Death is Life-
A Breath of God now Moved
Into a place of Inner Light
We've Moved INSIDE of You!

Man made in my 'Image'
Is Limitless like Me
Expressions of Our Linkage
To Connect Eternally!

So next time this 'Dis-Connection'
Called 'Death' feels lost-Unseen-
Remember Love's Perfection
Lives On IN You and Me!

"If Jesus Did Come Back Today...."

Don't you Wonder What He'd Say?
Would He agree with Companies
Who confess They Live His Way?

What would come First in His Works?
Would He be questioned in His Tracks?
Just like the Pharisees who plead
Rules behind His Back:

Like, reaching for the 'Clientelle'
Who appear to have more 'Class' -
Or would He reach for the hand that tells
Of Memories that last?

Would He make His Actions
Based on Fear how some may react?
Or would He make Reactions
From The Most Loving Facts?

Yes, History repeats Itself
When others Blind their View
God Help Us See How Jesus sees-
Not Crucify His Truth!

"If 'God IS Love,' how can He be 'Vengeful?'"

If Forgiveness is Real,
How can we stay 'Sinful?'

The Gift of Grace is our Miracle Healer.

Let No One deface A Child Of God.

"In The Shade"

So The Light keeps missing Where You Are-
And Dodging where you've been-
You stand upon The Stage to Start
And Try to Begin Again.

Standing Still, in Spotlight's aim-
In Hopes to share Its Light
Only to miss illusive Fame
As it slips way out of sight.

Do you Run or Do you Stay?
Prepare New Paths to take?
Or in a dim Acceptance Pray:
In Grace, Accept your Fate.

Until The Image on your Screen
Is Clear and Full of Light,
Others also cannot see
The Purpose for your Flight.

So Clear your Soul-
Clear your Heart-
Clear Out your Human Mind-
And Keep Your Sight
On The True and Right.
And Your Purpose You Will Find.
BE Now. BE Proud. BE Kind.

"In The Moment"

Moments come and Moments go-
As Quickly as Day to Night..
Good and Bad, some awkward, sad-
But they all affect our Sight.

What we 'See' May come and go-
But what remains is Clear:
It's not the Times that make us Kind-
It's LOVE that Transforms Fear.
When Hearts Connect-

God's Near.
Be IN The Moment- Be Here.

"In The Light of Fright"

No Dark Storm- No Missile Born
Can put out The White Light
No words that hurt can stop God's Bird
From Its Highest Flight...

The strain of Battle of Dark and Light:
The Oldest Story Told
May Pain The Gentle, Its stance may rattle -
But Strong God's Loving Hold.

Hang Tough, Dear Softest Heart and Soul
It's rough I know The Road...
But know Beside You, In His Hold
Is The Greatest Power Told

The Eternal Ne'er Will Fold.
LOVE Through ALL, God's Goal.

"It's The Climate Change" --

Of More Than Earth and Air!
It's The Climate Change -
Of More than Nature's Share...

It's The Change of Inner Weather
From Hot to Warm to Cold -
That makes a Person re-consider
His Conscience growing old.

Help Earth Be Immune, In Tune.
Help Humans Heal her with The Truth.

"From The Heart Led
To The Heartless"

Try as you might, Divisive Souls
Who hide Hate behind your Face -
You'll Never Defeat God's Ultimate Goal:
LOVE With ALL- No Race.

As we All come from The Same Creator,
And when sadly some Forget...
The Angel Forces, Sooner or Later
Will Reign Where God's Love Lives

Inside - One Life - God Gives.
Together Strong, LOVE IS.

Poems When Prayers Need Action:

"Mercy's Match"

Help Me Love More, God,
When my instinct is to Block-
Help Me Be More Open, God,
When I want to Stop the Clock.

Our only Protection from becoming Hate
Is Not To Hate the Hateful.
Our only Rejection is the Time we Wait
And become more like the Wasteful.

Have Mercy on our Merciless
Have Mercy on our Souls
But more-so Help when Mercy Tests
Our Hearts to Warm The Cold.

Help Us Live The Life You Told.
LOVE IS Olympic Gold.

"Living Real "

My Reality With You,
Is Better Than Dreams.
Right Here Right Now,
God's Son Light Beams:

Embrace The Sadness-
Embrace The Joy-
Embrace Each Moment
Life Employs.

Wrap our Hearts around Your Word-
Let Your Love Be All That's Heard.
Hug our Hearts So Deep Within-
We have no room for outer sin.
Your Pure Love, Our Soul Breathe In.
As Each New Day,
New Life Begins!

"To The Unexpected"

When Unexpected Tragedy-
Lights Up The Unknown-
It Wakes Up our Conscious Core Untouched-
In hidden Comfort Zones.

The Gift of Life's A Present-
More Precious could not be-
When we know our Lives are just Lent-
In our Trip through Eternity.

Peace we send to Life's Rude Awakenings-
When Life seems stopped Too Soon.
And Trust It Holds Inside an Opening -
As the Butterfly breaks Free the Cocoon.

Never ending...Re-Inventing Its Tune.
In the Darkness, Look Up to The Moon...
There's MORE to this Worldly Cartoon.

"Prayers for Divine Protection"
For What God Put Us For
Help Our High Intentions
See Only Blessings Soar.

Hurried Prayers Heal Hurricanes

We Call Upon The Angels
With Nature's Biggest Wings
To fly down fast and help the task
To Rescue Everything!

God Bless our Friends in our Great Land
As Neighbors We All Be
Protective Healing Prayers we lend
God's Miracles Be Seen....

Prayers for All That Be!

"In A World That Can Be Scary,"
We're Grateful for Sweet Souls
Who Remind us with their sensitive sharing-
Joy's a Heavenly Goal.
Live Love and you're never alone.

Kindness Blessings to your Day!

"Fast Moving Train"

So many scenes flash by our window
On this Fast Moving Train Called Life.
So fast, So full of places to go
Can't keep up with all the Sights.

I want to Stop, get off and drop
Into more scenes to play-
And yet this Train just moves so fast
I get lost along the way.

Guide me God.

"Hush the Rush"
Of Human Routine.....
Breathe Deep the Breath That Angels Sing
Fear Flies Away Upon Their Wings.

"When your Brain is Fried"
From Too Much Heat
And you need a Break to Breathe -
May these little Rhymes in Time
Cool your Inner Feet ...
Stroll in your Inner Breeze!
Keep Walking Towards Your Peace.

"Forgiveness is the fragrance
that the violet sheds on
the heel that has crushed it."
-- Mark Twain

"Comeuppance"

THIS is for The Dis-Respected
Those Over Looked and Feel Rejected,
Understand when some Think so Small
They Overlook The Spirits Tall...

This is for the Gifted Ones
Hurt by The Small in Power Runs,
Remember Your Higher Purpose Be
Higher than small minds perceive.

BLESS Them ALL!
Pray Healing Be!
Hold On To Light
To Be Set Free.

Forgive the Foot upon your head
And as the Violet,
God's Fragrance Shed.

The following Poem was written during my Telethon days, performing with my Mother. She would call these precious young souls with Cerebral Palsy "God's Special Children." This is dedicated to them and those of you with children dealing with such challenges in this life. You are Truly "God's Special Families." Angels Among Us.....

"All She Needs Is A Voice"

A little Child of Wandering Eyes
In a Prison of Bone and Flesh-
With Passioned Fervor, She's Life's Observer,
With Thoughts Longed to Express.

Sitting on my Lap, I felt,
This Little Child is Me....
Reflecting Longings Yet to Tell-
I Limit, too, what's seen.

Deep in those Eyes are Tender Cries
For Love, With Joyful Pleas-
The Form she takes, Flesh Prision Makes...
Surrounding A Soul Like Me.

All She Needs Is A Voice to Free
Her from a Muffled World,
All She Needs Is the Chance to Be
True Spirit - No Broken Girl.

"I'm more than 'Form' of Flesh and Bones,
Not "Handicapped" This Heart!
I'm More than a Voice through a Phone-
For "Spirit-Capped" we Are!

The Voice Inside of Me Transcends
The Body I'm Strapped In-
All I need is a Chance to Give
The Love Put Here To send..."

All She Needs Is a Voice To Free
For Flesh to Fly Above...
To Grow from Spirit's Holy Seed,
All She Needs Is LOVE!

IN
The Following Pages:

"Special Days and Holidays"
Are Markers In Our Lives-
Reminding Us to Remember Ways
Our Loved Ones Helped Us Rise....

May These Rhymes of Special Times
Bless Your Special Events-
As God Reminds With Special Signs:
Relish Each Moment Spent!

"Turning of Age"
(For a Teen's New Page)

No 1: A Wish for All That's True
    May your TeenAge years Inspire You!
No 2: A Wish for All That's Joy
    To Keep your Beautiful Smile employed!
No 3: A Wish for the Beauty you Are
    Inside and Out, Shining Near and Far
No 4: A Wish for Laughter Great
    Just like the kind you Give each day!
No 5: A Wish to Celebrate
    Discoveries each New Day your way!
No 6: A Wish for Patience, too
    Understanding Discoveries which com to you!
No 7: A Wish for Courage shown
    Each time you dare to Grow and Glow!
No 8: A Wish for Silly Times
    Remembering the 'kid' still lives inside!
No 9: A Wish for Open Mind Contemplating New
    Thoughts which you will Find!
No 10: A Wish for Open Heart
    Relishing New Feelings of Who You Are!
No 11: A Wish for New Ways to view
    Interpreting New Things that come to you!
No 12: A Wish for New Ventures pursued
    Expressing New Talents you grow into!
No 13: The Most Important Wish by far:
    A Wish that you'll remember How Loved You Are
    .... So that As you Grow through these years to be
    You Shine God's Gifts and Abilities!

(Originally Dedicated to Anabel Prince's
'AnabelAbility,' from her Grandpa and me :)

"Greater love hath no man than this, that a
man lay down his life for his friends."
-- John 15:13 King James Version

"A Day Of Honor"

Memorial Day-
A Day of Honor
Remembering The Best of Us.
Memorial Day-
A Day of Wonder
Of The Brave, The True, The Just.

Through all our Special Holidays-
The Get Togethers and Such,
May we not forget The Ways
Our Heroes Died for Us.

Rest In Peace, Dear Ones
We Owe Our Lives- Our Love.

"In His Service"

When we say "Thank You For Your Service,"
Deserving So Much More,
We Pray for Healing and your world Be Blessed
With Never Another War.

We Pray for Peace from
Memories that haunt so many fought.
For those come Home who Need More Help
To adjust what conflict's wrought.

We Pray that You Get Back To You
Moments taken from your Life-
Through Mankind's greed fulfilling needs
Causing Human Strife.

We Pray for The Brave
Who To This Day
Stand for The Good and True
May God Reward when Angels say:
"Welcome Home, Your Mission's Through."
God Bless Our Vets of Truth.
How We Love and Honor You!

In Honor of Memorial Day:

Its meaning is sobering....those who have
fallen to keep our Freedom.

A symbolic gesture to remind us each day of
the Preciousness Of Peace.

God Bless the Brave Souls who gave the
Ultimate Sacrifice for what they believed in.

May we live each day in the Awareness of the
never ending war between the Ego and the
Holy Spirit in our every day world. We have a
choice:

>   To Free our Lives,
>   we must Free our Spirits.

To The Best: Our Vets

To The Heart Of Every Veteran:
Our Gratitude we send
For a Mission Of Dedication-
For our Country you Defend.

We Pray God's Angels Defend You Too
And Give Back The Peace You Give -
And Salute With Wings Of Freedom-
The Brave Life You Have Lived.

This Veteran's Day reminds us all
How Honor never fades....
It just gets Brighter as each day falls
In Freedom that's been made...
By The Bravest Souls who keep the Goal
That Higher Service prays
That we remember our Freedom Senders
Long Live our Veterans' Days!

293

CONNIE FREEMAN PRINCE

"For This Day In Our World"
(9-11 and Beyond ...)

Another Anniversary
Reminders in our world
Of how this life's adversities
Oft set our News awhirl...

What can we do to right the wrongs
What can we do to heal
The suffering that lasts so long
That shakes our sense of 'Real'

Help us God to Remember
Your Great Teacher's Path to Change
Taught not the Path of war and hate
That Peace is Still in range...

But it Must Begin Inside of Us
In our daily 'wars' in life.
It Must Begin at The Source of Trust
When overcome by strife.

The Source of Life just sits and waits
For us to Re-Connect-
It's we who look for 'future dates'
When Now is our true test...

Right Now Inside to Heal our past
Begins with Letting Go
Of Hurt and Blame that only casts
Its web back where it's thrown.

We Surrender all the 'Hows' to You
Great Spirit Who brought us here
We surrender to Love's Healing Hue
To cast out doubt and fear.

Pour upon mankind your potion
Compassion yearns to flow
Into the cracks of bruised emotion
To Heal where hate may grow.

We become our blame to others
Their poison's double edged
For what we feel towards Any brother
Comes back to us and fed.

So we Surrender to The Greatest Healer
The Unforgivable
To The Promise made in His Greatest Pain
Love IS Retrievable.

God help us Be Your Hands and Feet
Now healed from piercing pain
And Hold Them Out With Love to Greet
The Only Path to Sane!

"Healing We Pray For Our Country"

Healing we pray for ourselves
For ultimately we are reflecting
What's in our souls to tell.

We pray for Human Kindness,
Compassion through the pain
Of realizing the Heartless need
Prayer more than disdain.

We pray for Miracles in these times
Of frightening human scenes -
And pray God's Grace takes the place
Of less than Love we see.

Forge on no matter what appears
Less than what we prayed -
For Ultimately we become
What We Think Each Day.

"For The Winded"

The Fragility of Life on Earth-
    We're reminded in Times like These.
        The Tragedies of lives so hurt
            By Life's Uncertainties.

We're Reminded The RESILIENCY
    Of the Human Spirit Strong-
        To Rally Round Where e'er they're Found-
            To Comfort what's gone wrong.

Angels Rally Round our Friends
    And Help them Rise Above-
        Reminding Us to Keep Our Trust:

What Lasts Through ALL is LOVE.

"God Speed to All Our Beloved Ones"
In Harm's Way right now:
Let Prayers on Angels Wings Unseen
Temper Storms All Around.

When Fear Leads...
Each Breath that's Breathed
In Faith, Will find refuge.
Let Safety Be With All You See -
Only Angels Fly With You!

Each Breath Breathed in Faith
Protects us All in Love.
Each Breath Breathed in Faith
Protects from Up Above.

Each Breath Breathed in Faith
God's Love is All Made Of.
Centered in Peace-It's Peace That We Be.
God Protects Us In His Love.

Prayers of Peace and Protection for you All!

Love Surrounding~~~

This Poem was written on a date that is now remembered in Prayers for Healing across our Country. Knowing I had to go out and 'Make people Laugh' in my job, hit me hard. I prayed for Appropriate Words to say and sing. The following words I feel my Angels sent to me help me go on....

I pray for Comforting Blessings to You and Yours as well --
From 9-11 and Beyond ...

"A Day With Sobering Reflections"
That comes by every year
Questioning life's rejections
Bringing up old fears...

Then Life Goes On.... but with different tones
When loss comes over us
We must remember we're not alone
When the sad makes friends with Trust.

As today I put on my "Lilly" Hat
With my Job of Bringing Joy
I'm reminded of Many Tragedies
Where Humor might annoy.

Then it came to me how the Depth of Life
Encompasses Grief with Laughter
For if we Truly Believe through strife
There's Heaven in Ever After...

So, this fateful date I post to you
My Heart's Compassion and......
The Thought that we are More in Truth
Held in God's Loving Hand.

Peace, More Peace and Then Peace Again...
Our Prayer for All On Earth -
With Testament through each lament,
On the Other Side, There's Mirth!

Our Goal for Comfort from Heaven to Earth
Reflects on days like this:

That No Man can kill us with Human Hurt,

For in the End –

LOVE IS ALL THERE IS.

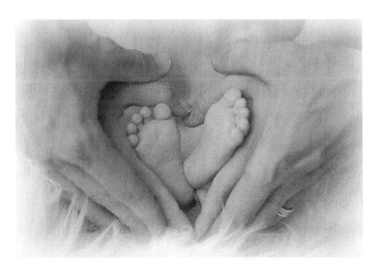

"Happy Independence Day!"

Dear God, What are we 'Independent' from?
Help our Independence Be-
Remembrance from where we came from,
Our Heritage let see.....

Freedom from Intolerance
Freedom from Dis-Grace
Freedom to Express the Heart
And Soul of this Blessed Place!

May this Birthday of America
Re-New our Memory Of
Our Founding Fathers
Who Like None Other
Stood Up for What We Love:

Freedom of Expression
Freedom to Believe
In God We Trust
Stand Over Us:
The Brave, The True, The WE!
God Bless The True America!
Please Heal With Love That Frees!

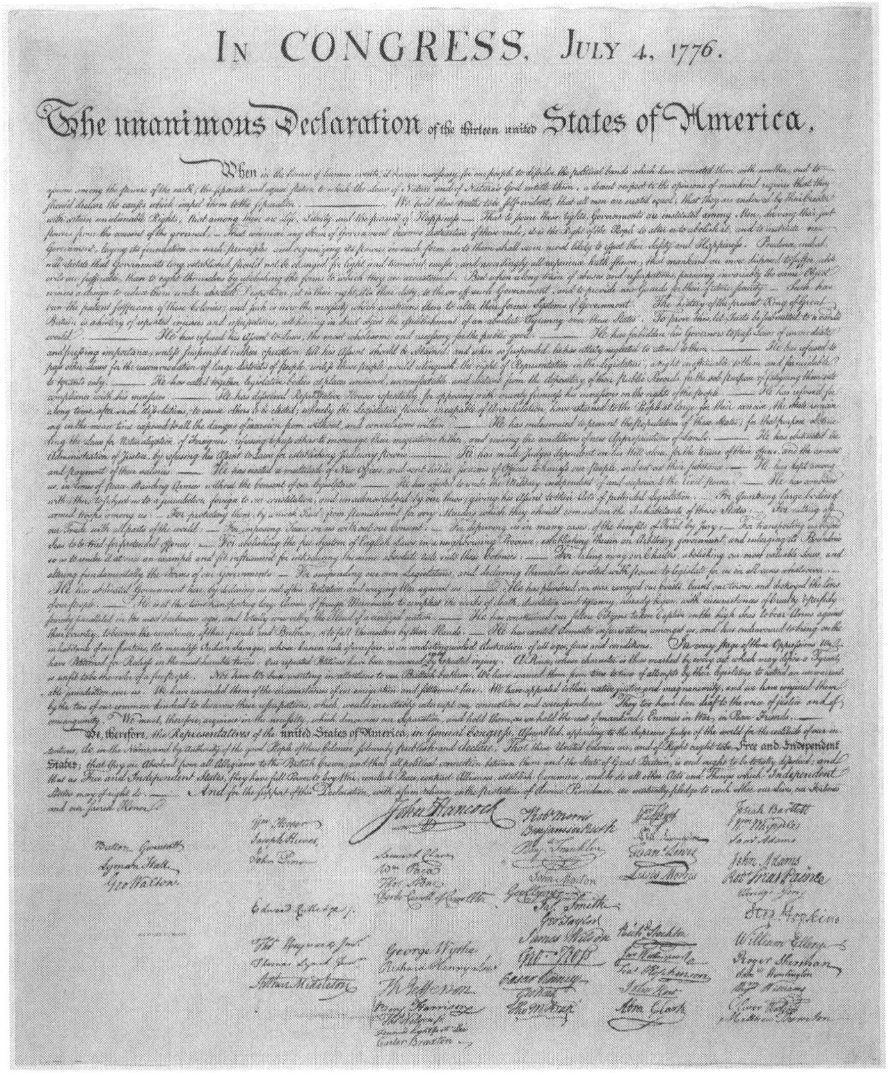

IN CONGRESS, JULY 4, 1776.

The unanimous Declaration of the thirteen united States of America,

"A Crucial Prayer for Crucial Times"

Dear God,

Please Protect Us
From the 'Well Intentioned Insane'
Who attack in our 'Free' Country
For standing up against the grain.

Dear God Please Deliver Us
From these Times of Cruelty
Projecting 'Political Correctness'
In place of Sanity.

Let not History Repeat Itself-
With Brother Against Brother-
When Freedom of Speech was stilted
By disguised Dictators.

The scariest part is when you see
Those you Love so blinded
By the need to 'Prove they're Right'-
Even when New Truths are sighted.

Heal Our Country and Its People
As More Scary News they show-
We are praying for a Miracle-
To Heal our Country's Soul.

"Thousands of candles can be lighted from a single candle, and the life of the candle will not be shortened. Happiness never decreases by being shared."

~ Buddha

"The Light of Peace"

Now more than ever, we must join with The Great Light our Souls came from to help Heal those in darkness. Prayers of Healing Peace-filled Light surround ALL Around The World!

Love & Peace Angels We Call Upon~~~

Perfect Love and Faith, Lit from Within, Still Has The Power To Cast Out Fear.

Divine Guidance we pray for all of our Leaders.

Divine Outworking we pray for each of us in our daily lives.

"A Mother's Heart"

The Heart of God -
The Creator of All Things-
If All the world could Feel That Love,
The saddest Heart would Sing!

For all The Moms, near and far-
Both Heaven and on Earth,
In Deepest Gratitude we are
For Your Healing when Life Hurts-

Your Love, Organic, Deep and True
Is the Heart of Purest Love
Happy Mother's Day to You!
Angel Blessings from Above.

"God Bless the Mother Spirits"

Who nurture the Souls of All!
They come to earth with Angel Wings
To catch us when we fall~

We Give Thanks Today for Each of You
With Unconditional Love,
Reminding us of What Is True:
Soul Love from Up Above!

"In Honor of A Mother's Love"

When One thinks of God -
Where We All Come From.....
One Vision comes to mind:
Reflections of A Mother's Love-

The Birth of Human Kind.
No Greater Love To Find...
God's Love: A Mother's Truth!
Each Day God Loves Through You!

"The Shell Must Break Before the Egg must Fly"
                                        - Tennyson

"Happy Mama Hen Day!"
(a message from 'The Poultry Gates' :)

When God needed His Arms in Flesh
To comfort newborn souls,
He remembered who Loved his Son the best:
His Mother, a Saint untold.

His Arms, His Hands, His Heart, His Life
Breathed into Human Form,
Could not have happened without this Bright
Light we all adore!

To all the Mothers who share their lives
With all their Hearts we say:
Thank You for being our Spirit Guides
God Bless this Mother's Day!

In Honor Of Mother Earth Day

"Earth to People! Earth to People!
Will You Come In Please?"
Said Mother Earth to her 'Guests,'
On This Planet Needing Peace

"Is Anybody Home Here on my Holy Ground?
Are Any of You Still Aware We Need Your Care Profound?"

Mother's Day for Mother Earth
Needs more than just One Day
It needs Appreciation Heard
It needs us All to Pray...

That All the Climates of this World
Find Control in Consciousness
It's All Connected- As Thoughts Converge
As Good and Bad contests.

Our Earthly Home Reflects the Tone
Of Mankind's State of Being
Dear God Help Heal what we've been shone
And Honor Earth's Deep Meaning.

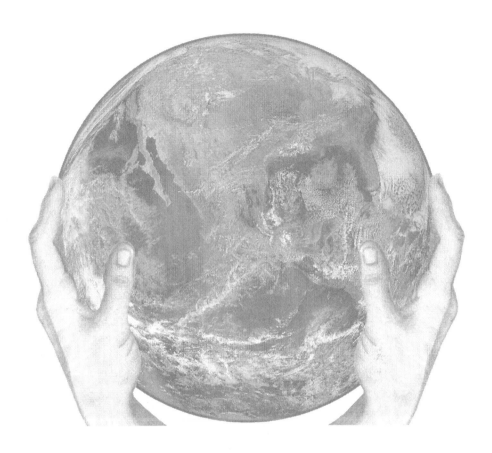

"A Letter to Our Mother"
(On The Anniversary of Her Death)

Thank You For Our Life
That Breathed Life Into Me
We would not be here, lest for You-
Because of You We See.

Thank You For Your Life
For The Life You Gave to All
Our Siblings and Their Children
Are here cause of Your Call.

When a First Generation leaves us
It's Sobering to our Soul,
When Life Goes On, it Grieves Us-
Yet Wakes Us To God's Goal.

Of Carrying On HIS 'Mission'
One Generation to the next-
You Left us with Tradition
And Creation at Its Best.

Thank You For Our Lives
That would not have happened without You.
And the thousands that you touched in kind
Fare Better for Your Truth ...

We Feel You Deeply On This Day
Even More Than e'er before-
You're in our Blood, in our Ways
We Think and Feel Life More.

There Is No Death
Just Transition-
We Live It Every Day.
Each second, minute, moment passes
Gives rise to Life's New Ways.

Thank You for New Life in You,
Dear Father Who Made Us All.
Fly Well to Your New Life in Truth
We Carry On Your Call
Though We Miss You Most of All.

In Honor of All Mothers

Moments:

This photo is a Remembrance of a Special Moment with our Mom, Doris "Cousin Tuny" Freeman, when she received the "Woman of The Year" Award in Jackson, TN in 1963. Surrounded by "Yours Truly" (her youngest) and my siblings Cindie, Pat and Jim. We still Remember how a Mother's Embrace is Timeless.

In Honor of International Women's Day"

To The Women of our World each day-
Where we come from Is The Womb they prayed.
Strong in the Deepest of Man's Human Ways
Who keep us all going- Always deserving more pay!

Rally round and lend your ears-
As Mother Nature and Earth Appears!

No matter the Distance- No matter the Dance-
They sense how we Feel & leap for the Chance....

Through All Walks of Life
Let History take note
Though kept out of sight-
Still- New Chapters they wrote....

The Calling to bring Peace to the World-
Is The Feminine Nature that Nurture unfurls.
For without The Original Mother of Love,
There would not be a Savior
Brought to earth from Above!

God Bless The Power of Original Life, God calls Woman!

International
Women's Day
Festival

"In Honor of Teachers"

With Greatest Blessings and Gratitude!

And God said:
He must send down some
Guidance-

For Growing Souls within the world-
So many things they need to learn- every boy and girl.

It must be a Special Calling -
Withstanding pay and care.
And be Beyond all Falling-
And the Highest Standards share...

Beyond your standard Angels-
Or understanding Preachers-
Their Mission Great and Faithful:
That's Why God Created Teachers.

"Father Day Poem"

To all The Dads
Our Hearts are Glad
To celebrate this day!
Your Strong Wings
That help us sing
Protected as we play.

And to those who've earned their wings in Heaven,
Like mine I miss today....
We send our Thoughts to Fly with you
In The Land where Spirit Plays....

Thank You for still looking after us
Thank You, we know you're There
And our Greatest Thanks to our Eternal One
Our Father's Love we share.

"A 'Father's Day' Prayer"

"Our Father, Which Art In Heaven"
How we need you This Father's Day-
Your Strength, on Wings of Angels-
Give Comfort to All Who Pray.

Help soothe this world's rough edges-
That bruise the softest Hearts.
Help make us Strong, as we Belong
In The Heart of Who You Are.

This Father's Day, we Thank our Father Figures Near and Far-
And Remember we are Sisters, Brothers
In Our Heavenly Father's Heart.
Help Us Be The Love You Are.

"Father's Day Thoughts...."

Dear Father of us All,
Help us to Give Your Mercy
When those around us fall...

In a world where Human Kindness
Is replaced with Ego Greed,
Help us see Beyond the Blindness
Of Souls Who Cannot See...

That Every One's a Father-
A Mother in their way-
Help us Remember ALL Are Brothers
On a Heavenly Father's Day.

"Labor" Day
(Food for Thought to Hatch)

We're All In Labor
Giving Birth
To New Life every day
Through All Hurt- Through All Mirth
We have to Find A Way...

Through This Birth Canal called Life
Through each working day
Until we find it's worth the fight
To Turn All Work To Play!

Life is Precious
Water Breaks
And Sometimes, So Do We-
But we Take a Breath,
We Reach New Depths
To Love Eternally!

"Labors Of Love"

A Labor Intensive Journey
Into Why you were put here:
Your Work is Deeper than you See-
It transcends every fear.

Labor Pains in daily life
Are Spirit Muscles stretched
Around your Soul to make you Go
To Reach Your Very Best.

We Each Have a Special Mission
Since the Day our Lives Began...
What Brings You Joy and feeds your Passion?
That's Your Purpose, Friend!

"Come September Song"

Sing Inside Our Hearts!
So Sweetly and Sincerely...
New Seasons Share Their Art..
Through Nature, sometimes fiercely.

And Bring New Healing Peace
To Each Heart bruised today
"This Too Shall Pass"
Let No Storm Last-
Help Love To Find Its Way!

Heal This Fall We Pray!
Come September, Play!

"Autumn Reverie"

A Tree Alive With Autumn leaves
Golden in the sun
Rustled with the wind's soft breeze
Invisible, Its Touch...

Then the Peaceful Place That Filled me,
Bonded with those Leaves:
Moved by Energies Unseen,
Touched by Nature's Weave....

Weaving in the The Tapestry-
All Connected We...
When One Leaf Leaves, the others weep-
Then Reunite in Spring.

315

"Happy Autumn Equinox!"

First Day of Fall!
First Day to Rise!
To Unpredictable Calls
In this Adventure known as LIFE!
Nature Gives Her All...

The Temps Uncharacteristic -
The Events could challenge a Mystic
But Deep Inside Still Resides
A Power
Of Faith Realistic!

So we Greet New Seasons calling us...
To Awaken with Great Care-
And Focus LOVE in All of Us
Our Destiny's Still There!

Color To Your EveryWhere!

"On This Hallow's Eve"

Through times we grieve
Reminds us Still to chill
Perception's key - in times like these:
Of the Potpourri we feel:

This Life's a Mix
Of 'Treats and Tricks'
Of Sadness and of Joy-
And the Child Within
Still yearns to lend
Its whims of Hope employ.

So we Stand Up to pain with tears some days-
And others, laughter through -
Remembering when Fears re-gain
God's Joy Lives On In Truth!
Happy Halloween to you!

"Happy Daylight 'Saving Time'"

As we 'Fall Back' with Another Hour-
May we Breathe More Life In Thee...
Catch A Breath in the Rush that showers
Every Day we see.

Reminded of the Preciousness
Of Each Hour On this Earth.
How Important Each Impression Is-
Of The Energy We Serve.

Thank You for this 'Extra Hour'-
May we Take For Granted None.
And Remember that it's Up to Us
How We Rise Up With The Sun!

May we Save More Time for Love.

Happy Day 'Life Saving'Time

I "Fall Back" Through The Wings of Time...
Flying way too fast-
I Fall Back Through These Daily Signs ...
Asking, 'Will This Last?'

The Answer then Flew back to me
As fast as The Clock it plays:
Focus Not on The Time that flees-
Focus On This Day.

The Time Is NOW - Fly Brave!

"Where Thanks Needs Giving"

In a world where Thanks Needs Giving
Amidst all Humans Hurt
We're reminded Why we're Living
And brought Here down to Earth.

God needs our Hearts, our Hands for Art
The Art of Living Love.
It's up to us to play our parts
Annointed from Above.

So This ThanksGiving, My Heart is Full
Of Love and Thanks for YOU
Through Time and Space, none can erase
Connections made in Truth.

Thank You Thank You from my Soul
Thanks to God Above
Who Reminds us we were Born to Glow
To Shine His Healing Love....

"Give Thanks In All Circumstances"
A Serving of Peace Pie

"Give thanks in all circumstances;
for this is the will of God in Christ Jesus for you."
1 Thessalonians 5:18

It's easy to Give Thanks-
For those you Love each day.
For Family and Close Friends
Who see Things agreed your way.

But what about 'All Circumstances'-
Even those that cause you pain?
And those whose words may pierce your Heart
And threaten your domain?

It's been said when you Block your Heart,
You Block a part of God,
So Giving Thanks can oft feel hard,
When things challenge Who You Are.

Giving Thanks Anyway
Gives you back your Power-
Replacing Anger with Compassion
In your darkest hour.

Give Thanks because it shows you
What's weak Inside your Soul-
Give Thanks because it knows Truth
And how to make you Whole.

To 'Give Thanks in Every Circumstance'-
Regardless good or bad-
Is The Path to Peace Released
In a world down cast.

A Salve to Soothe your Soul.
Give Thanks And Watch Life Grow!

The Power of 'Thanks Giving'
My Wish for You

What Do We Give Thanks for?
We're Reminded This Great Day-
The Power of Great Gratitude
Can help Heal Human Ways...

The Power of a 'Thank You'
Is Greater than we know!
It re-enforces Love and Truth
For what we Think, Will Grow....

So we Thank You, God,
As for ALL we Pray:
For ALL Below, Above-
We Thank You God as we Learn to Play
Your 'Thank You Note' ♪
Of LOVE!

♪"A Note Of Thanks"♪

Thank You from my Heart So Full
Of Gratitude For You
Life's a Birth Day Every Day
With Angels Living True

Through Rains and Storms
Since we've been Born,
Our Lifeboats get us Through
And Sail Above With Joy and Love
On the Seas Of Gratitude.

I Thank God For You!

"Hugs for The Holidays"

It's A Moment!
Catch it before it goes...
Slipping through the cracks of Time-
Gone before you know.

It's A Moment!
Relish every second
Living Awareness In This Now-
Is The Key of Love that beckons...

When Life is filled with Rushing Around,
Let One Moment Stop In Time-
And Remind us Greatest Joy Is Found
In The Moment-
Peace Abounds

God's Love Is All Around!

I'm So Grateful for Special Moments Like These!

Connie & Bobby

'Twas The Week Before Christmas...."

...And all through the Earth
Amidst all the Wishes
Are Humans who hurt.

As the countdown begins
For The Christ Who Transcends
God Help Us Forgive
Please Help Us To Mend.

The Broken, The Sad,
In this time to be Glad
If others have hurt us,
Transcend fromthe bad.

When others ignore
Your Healing Love Saves,
Rebirth and Restore
Please show us Your Grace.

Help us Forgive
And Let it All Go
For Peace on this earth
Begins Here At Home.

As our Savior was Born
In the Humblest of ways,
So our Souls must Transform
In our own Christmas Days.

"Christ Child Re-Born"

Christ Be Born Inside Of Us!
Be Born Pure Love, Pure Light-
Be Born Pure Peace That We Can Trust
To See All Through Your Sight ...

The Birth Of Christ
Is The Birth Of Hope-
That LOVE Turns Wrongs To Right.
Let His Connection Deeply Flow
To Give Your Heart New Life!

Merry Christmas Bright!!

"Christmas Hope"

Hooray...The World Is Still Here!
ReBorn this Christmas Time!
Amidst a time of doubts and fears,
It Reminds us to be Kind~

As that little Babe of humble means
Showed us all The Way....
So His Love remains- what e'er the change,
Christmas Be Each Day!

Happy Christmas into your New Year Blessings!!!

"The Snow of Silent Recovery..."

After the Raging Fires of Life
After the Rusting Rains of Strife-
We're Stopped within our Tracks.

Too Cold to look back
Too tired to fight ....
A Blanket of Snow
A Heavenly Sight-

A Blanket to Silence the Hurry of Life
A Silence we're given to Calm in the Night.
To Calm how we're livin'
Sweet Peace we are given.
We Breathe in the Silence so Still -

The Breath of a Bird
Hidden Nest far away
So Silent and Still -
- It stops here to Pray.

As the Earth Breathes in Snow
So Thirsty Today.
So thirsty for Peace
Pure White Sparkling Sheen.
Please wipe our slates Clean-
This First New Year's We See -
Help Us to Breathe your Sweet Purity.

"Back to The Present"

Time Traveling
In The Dimensions-
Deep Inside my Head...
Mixtures of The Past & Present-
And Places I've been Led.

I fight The Flight to Future-
Knowing THAT I can't control-
And yet Each Moment Endured
Is a Trip Inside my Soul.

Back to Present-
Back to Now-
A Round Trip Ticket to Peace...
Reminds me the Only Time that's Real
Is The Now that does not cease.

Put your Wanderlust At Ease.
Unwrap The Present:
God's Gift To Peace.

"New Year Musings"

What's New about This New Year's?
What's New Begins With You:
Have you let go of last year's fears?
If you have, Then You'll Be New!

Each Year, Each Day, Each Minute
LIfe Begins Anew
But whether or not you LIVE It
Is entirely up to You.....

Happy New Year Blessings!
Blessed we are to say
Each Breath We Take, Each Prayer We Make
Makes Each Day New Year's Day!

May Your Year Be Blessed
With All That Inspires Your Heart To Dance!

"My New Year's Resolution"
...Is to Surrender each Solution
To Higher Power that Knows The Best for All~

To Focus Thoughts on Gratitude-
To Transform Every Attitude-
Into Light when Darkness-
Hints that it may fall....

For The Greatest Lesson I've Learned So Far
In each New Year that's passed:
Is that Forgiveness is Your Healing Star
For Peace Within to Last~

As we Let Go of the year Before,
We Give Thanks for Brand New Doors
Ready to Open, Love is our Omen
To Fly with Faith that Soars!

"A Message to Eclipsing Moon"

Traveling by our Sun.....
When you cast your Shadow,
Help us View
Hopes Hidden Now Begun.

Shed Your Light Upon Our World
Help Wipe Away Our Blocks
To See New Light in Life Unfurl
To Heal our Human Flocks.

Let's Love With All We Got!

"Soul-er Eclipse"
(Signs of The Times)

As The Shadow of The Recent Moon
Revealed The Brightest Sun
So The Shadows in our lives will soon
Reveal New Life Begun.

We can choose to View The New
Through eyes of fear that burn
Or Look through Lens of Love and Truth
Revealing Lessons Learned...

See The Signs - See These Times
As Tickets to New Peace
Shadows scare- but pass with care...
If Only We Believe.

"Beyond The Ground Hog's Shadow"

And The Day Begins Again...
One foot in front of the other-
Sun Up to Descend-
Recycling for each brother...

Till the Ground Hog shows his shadow-
In the Comfort of Tradition,
We're reminded by what follows-
In our ever changing condition...

One foot in front of the other...
The Sun Still Rises, Friends!
As Awareness will uncover
This day will soon Transcend...

Routine gives way to Surprise
That Life is here to Lend
Evolving Wisdom to the Wise:
THIS Day won't come again!

Relish Each Moment, Friend!

"A Verse to 'Ground' your Day"

Will you see Your 'Shadow'
This Lovely Ground Hog's Day?
Predictions: Cold or soon Spring Meadows,
Perception Lights The Way...

Perceptions Turn Predictions
Into Good or Bad
Let Faith release your Heart's Restrictions
To Love Away The Sad...

A New Day Alive- Be Glad!!

A Grateful Valentine's
'Lessons from a Soul Mate'

LOVE
Sweet LOVE
Valentine's True LOVE
Is More than meets the Eye
It's the Essence of Where We Come From...
It's God's Deep Joy Inside.

I've learned how when we Deeply BE
That LOVE we wish to see
When we BE what our Hearts plead ...
We Live what Dreamers read.

For LOVE is More than Surface
That is, the Kind you Dream...
It comes from Depths where Angels wept
When Life's not what it seems.

It Withstands Pain of Human Gain-
It Lives through hurt and loss
It Rises Higher from where it came-
Grows Deeper from Its Cross.

LOVE
Sweet LOVE
Valentine's True LOVE
Romance of Heart and Soul
Turns Heartbreak into Laughter
Its Heaven makes us Whole!
May Our World Make Love its Goal!
Meet in The Center
Where Heaven can Enter
As True LOVE's what makes Life Glow!

"For Valentine's....."

As quickly as this world goes by
As news reflect, elections fly
This World Still Stops With Valentine's
Each Soul Still Yearns for Love so Kind.

So as this day, as Life flies by
Remember That Love Can Still Stop Time-
A Smile, A Hug, Still Makes Us Sigh~
The Power of Love is Valentine's!

"Valentine Verse"

In this month of Valentines,
May God's Love Within
Magnify All You Are
In Spirit we are Kin …

In this Life, True Love's The Best!
This Valentine's I send ...
The Love of Soul, An Angel Guest
To Light your Heart Within!

"Happy Heart and Valentine's Day"

May your Soul take Flight on Wings Above~
And Fly Within in Heavenly Love~
From Mine to Yours in rhyme I say:
Happy Heart and Valentine's Day!

"LOVE -- What Gives Us Breath"
(A Valentine's Heart Card for You)

LOVE:
  -What Gives Us Breath

  LOVE:
    -What Takes It Away

    LOVE:
      -Life At Its Best

      LOVE:
        -We Pray Will Stay

This Valentines in a world so mixed
With Heart and Heart Breaking News
May This Day of Love Remind us of
Romance Which Lives In Truth.

Romance Your Life In Love Each Day
Romance Your Power To BE
A Walking Breathing LIGHT of LOVE:
The Air Your Spirit Needs!

Breathe In This Love This Special Time
Breathe Deep Right Now....... and See
The Deepest Love This Valentines
Is The Soul of You and Me.

Ahh......

To Be in the Blue

To Be in the Waves

Washing away all the cares of this day....

Away......In the Blue.....

With You....

Ahh.....

To Be Free ......

To Feel the Peace Of Nothing to Do but Be in the Blue......

With You.....

Away with the Waves in the Blue....

Ahh......

To Be Floating On The Flow Of the Waves

Of Peace and Beauty and Love Of Nature's Song...

Of Nature's Blue....

Ahh..... to Be Flying

To Be Soaring On A Wave

Of Tranquility and Blue and You....

No Cares. No Worries.

Just Blue....

With You.....

Washing Away In The Blue

Floating Away.....

Flying Away......

Soaring Away

Above the world

On the Waves

In The Blue

In The Love

In The Peace

Sweet Peace

Joyful Peace

Escaping this world

With You......

In the Blue ....

"To The Ashes"

To the Ashes on this Wednesday-
This First day of Lent-
What shall I Give Up? What shall I Pray?
In this world where Hope's been spent.

Giving Up the Giving Up
Giving Up lamenting
Giving Up the Giving Up
In Life that's Everlasting

Help us Fast from fast fear thoughts
Bombarded from Mankind
And Slow Them Down with Wisdom taught
By Sages throughout Time....

Dust to Dust- Ash to Ash-
But Wait -- We're All Still Here!
Just Another Reminder
For All to Be Kinder
Let Grace Replace All Fears.

Pure Love Holds Angels Near!

"Holy Week"

A 'Palm Sunday' of Sundays

As Palm Sunday begins this Holy Week,
This Holy Week in Time,
A Time we've never seen before --
Still God's Promise Speaks Sublime!

So..... If you happen to Wonder-
When Appearance speaks Thunder-
Remember Love's Story of Glory:
A Promise To Rise - In front of our Eyes-
Our Prayers He is Not Ignoring....

Hold On, when on the Outside
Uncertainty abides-
Hold On, in just A Matter of Time,
We're Promised We Too Salvation will find...
And from the Ashes We'll Rise!

Hold On!

Peace and Love to you, my sweet Spirit Friends!!

335

"What Is 'Good' In Good Friday?"

What Is The 'Good' in Good Friday?
What is The Good in Pain?
When it appears all The Love that you Gave
Was taken -- by the Insane?

What is Important to some
Is looked down on by others.
When your Light Gets Too Bright,
They Dim -

Yet The Greatest of These
Brings despair to its knees,
When The Greatest of These you Live.

So we Live in the Faith of these Fateful Three Days
Before The Son Rises Again.
Have Mercy On All, our Deep Human Call:
Into God's Hands We Transcend!

An Easter Reflection...

Life's "Three Days Before Your Resurrection"

"O Father, Where Art Thou?"

There Comes a Time when Faith Grows Up
Into a Knowing Being
A Knowing Deep Inside Your Soul
That transcends mere 'Believing'

You Know By Breathing In Sweet Air
It's not that you 'Believe'
It's Becoming One: One With Your Prayer
It's Knowing God Won't Leave...

It's In Your Bones You're Not Alone
The Kingdom of God Is HERE!
As Close as the "i" in your iPhone
So Close, It's More Than Near...

So when you're feeling Out of Breath-
Out of life's reserves-
A soul burned out in the midst of tests,
Stop - INHALE God's Word...

It's Spiritual Oxygen this world craves
Unknowingly breathing air
Polluted by uncaring slaves
To ego driven care.

Breathe, Rest and Wait Three Days
Three Minutes, Three Years? The same.
For in the end all Time will blend
Into THIS Moment of Grace~

THIS Moment is IT!
It holds the Seed of Resurrecting Grace
But first you must Wake Up and get
OUT of the Grave you're in...

Dig Deep and Become Unburied
From Earth that's masked your eyes
Dig Deep and See Inside you've carried
The Means from which to Rise!

Eastertime is Every Time
We Wake Up to God Within...
Rise Up to LOVE! With LOVE You'll Find
New Life Begins Again!

"It's Our Sweet Easter Rising"

It's our Sweet Rising Time of Hope
It's our Sweet Easter Rising
Inside our Savior takes us Home
What a Divine Timing!

So if you're Feeling Sad and Lonely
And you don't know which way to go
Then it's Time for your Easter Rising
Just ask sweet Jesus Raise Your Soul.

"Easter Blessings"

The Greatest Message Known To Man-
The Greatest Hope E'er Given:
How God Can Take The Worst of Plans
And Transform Death To Livin!

What e'er The Cross You Bear Today-
Take Heart- Take Heed- Take Hope!
For through your pain, LOVE Finds A Way
Take Hold This Holy Rope!

Hold On- Press On- Surrender Son
And when your Heart feels torn-
Remember New Life's Just Begun...
Praise God, There's Easter Morn!!

The Unknown Story of the Lost Little Easter Egg

And The Easter Egg said:

"Will Anyone Ever Find Me??
I've been hiding here so long
They seem to walk right by me
And even mow the lawn!

Will Anyone Ever Find Me??
My shell is getting worn
By years of waiting to be seen
My Inner Yolk's forlorn :(

And Then after years of waiting
For Someone Else to come
She remembered her friend the Butterfly
Discovered Her Own Sun!

The Butterfly broke out of Her Shell
Not waiting for someone else
To Discover her wings with story to tell
She listened to her 'Inner Bell'

So the little egg listened well
Inside where Truth & Wisdom dwells
And felt a stirring Within her Shell
That she was born with a story to tell!

So she waited no more to be 'Discovered'
She had to 'Discover' Her Self
She had to Dis-cover what fear had kept covered
From fear what others would tell...

And then she realized the shell around others
Had nothing to do with hers
How could They uncover - when Theirs they had smothered
Being planted too far under Earth?

So by following the lead of her Butterfly Friend
She hatched for all she was worth
Though still runny her yolk, the Sun finally broke
And Baked her into Pure Mirth!

So now she lives quite Sunny Side Up
As she's Living Her Story to Tell
And This Easter Egg Hunt had only begun
As She Finally Broke Out of Her Shell!

Happy Easter Rising Time!!

339

"Just remember in the winter, far beneath the bitter snows Lies the seed, that with the sun's love in the spring becomes the rose."

-- Amanda McBroom

Happy Birth of Spring!!

As Winter Moves Over,
Uncertain the Air-
Yet the Promise of Spring
Still Arrives Everywhere!

As "The Rose" sweetly says:
In the Coldest Distress,
New Seasons Still Bless
Mother Nature's New Dress!

So Put New Springs in Your Step-
New Hope in your Play --
Have Faith for New Life
For A New Brighter Day!

"Daylight Saving Mankind Time"

Daylight Savings Time!
Save Another Hour...
Moving quickly through our lives-
Help Us, Higher Power!

Marking Time of Mankind
Is like holding onto clouds
Passing way Too quickly
Before Its Truth is found....

BREATHE This Week
DEEP in Spring
Even through the Cold
While Springing Forward, Peace we seek
This Present Moment: Gold!

"Daylight Savings Welcome!"

Daylight Savings Time Is Here!
Springing Forward Into Cheer!
As New Flowers Bloom New Hope...
C'mon Spring, Let's Warm The Cold!

Time To Heal With Love That Grows!

"Springing Forward"

Springing Forward Into Joy-
Let the Hour gently pass.
Nature has her way of Changing
Future into Past...

Seize the Hour, Seize The Moment
Each One Will Bring New Life
Better Days are on their Way...
When we Clarify our Sight:

See the Sunrise and Sunsets
As Signs You'll Rise Again!
When we Choose to See The Best,
Then Time Becomes Our Friend.

New Season-
Love ... Transcend!

"Spring Time Hope"

May your Hearts be filled with Springtime Hope!

May your Souls be Filled Love~

May this Month of May Bring Joy each day...

"Connections" from Above!

"Lost & Found"

I was looking for that Hour We lost just yesterday-
Could it be in 'Storage' of old outdated plays?

Should I keep looking for What's Lost
And ne'er got done in time?
Or just pretend and wait till end
Of 'Daylight Savings Time?'

Then it occurred to me I 'lost'
Not one bit of 'Time.'
How can one lose what he never knew-
A Man Made Clock and Sign?

As The Sun Still Sets and Rises-
Never thinking what's left behind...
But what it needs to Light This Moment-
Ah, Nature knows This Rhyme:

Now Is Now
And Then Is Then
And Forever Breathes No Strife
In the Rhythm Of Nature's Prism-
Thus, The Hourglass Of Life.

"Happy April Fool's Day!!"

Are you Chicken?
Or Are you Duck?
Or Are you Human?
Then You're in Luck:

You have The Power to Change the Rules:
Be Who You Want:
It's April Fools!!

♪ "Though April Showers May Come Your Way-
You Have The Power to Make Your Day!
Like If It's Raining, no need regret:
Do not complain- just 'See' that Rain as Raining Chickenettes!
So if you see clouds, They Are Not Real
It's April Fool's Day
Time to Appeal:
And Look At Life Around You-
And Lighten Up Life's Song
Whenever April Fool's Day Comes Along!" ♪

"Unexpected Angels"

"World Down Syndrome Day"
IS "World Poetry Day" ....

In So Many Special Ways:
As The Love and Joy The Poets Say
Is The Life for which we Pray.

These Special Children and Their Kin
Are Examples of Great Love
We Celebrate what The Angels Sent
From The Sweetest from Above!

We Honor Y'all Today!!
And Grateful You came our way!

"In Honor of World Poetry Day"

This Life is a Rhyme
Of All Humankind
A Mixture of Verses
A Measure of Time...

That helps us to Focus
On Beauty and Truth
Life's Mystery Shows Us
The Poetic in You!

The Melody of Life
Be Blessed by this Play
Of Joy amidst strife-
World Poetry Each Day!

CONNIE FREEMAN PRINCE

"The Vagueness of Reality"

• • •

• • •

• • •

Index

For the Heart of Your Journey

Thanks and Acknowledgments

Every Soul Encounter on this earth contributes not only to Who we Become but also What we Do. There are not enough pages to include Each Person who has been Invaluable to me and to whom I will be Forever Grateful for on my Path to the printing of this book. I Hope You Know Who You Are Already. But since asked, for limited literary purposes and space, I must list the following to express my personal Gratitude:

• <u>First and Foremost, my Beloved Mr Prince</u> without whom the manifestation of this Book from my Soul would not have given birth. Little did I know when God had our Paths Magically Cross, The Way Was Being Paved in the Form of A Marriage to this Brilliant and Creative Mate of My Soul. Through the Surviving of Major Life Illnesses, we've faced Life and Death together and the uncertainties of every day existence, into the Unmapped world of Musical and Poetic Creations. We have parented Together our Life's Dreams. In helping to tirelessly design, organize, edit and arrange the format of this book, his Brilliance is matched only by his supportive creative feedback from the musical world he comes from. He is a Musical Pioneer in the Video Game Industry (Lifetime Achievement Award Winner), and is known world wide for his inventive Music and Sound Design, inspiring many young musicians today in that genre. I am so Honored and Inspired by his Professional and Personal Partnership, as he continues to create even more Musical Dreams and Creations. There are no words Deep Enough and No Rhyme Rich Enough to house my Soul Gratitude to him for finding me in these Ever Evolving Mountains of Life on Earth. My Love for you, my Real Life "Prince Charming," is Boundless. My Admiration for you: Astounding.

• <u>My Mother</u> was known to many in West Tennessee as the Legendary "Cousin Tuny," Star of her very own Live Children's TV Show in the Fifties and Sixties. One of the first women to be inducted into The Tennessee Radio Hall of Fame, she was a gifted Performer and Pioneer in the Industry. Her Philanthropic Heart helped to raise life changing funds on numerous Telethons helping Children with Cerebral Palsy (Page 148). She also partnered with Carl Perkins to raise funds for his Center for The Prevention of Child Abuse.

Growing Up around her working with Carl in those Telethon years, I learned from stories of her and Minnie Pearl, including many about Great Souls from my Hometown of Jackson, Tennessee.

Her poignant autobiography "Cuz," beautifully co-authored by my sister Cindie Haynie, is filled with such legendary experiences. One of those experiences I witnessed backstage at a Telethon, spoke more about her than my words can say. As stage hands were rushing by her getting ready to get back on the air, the world stopped when she spotted a little girl who was blind, and the girl asked her what she 'looked like.' Mother stopped everything, knelt down and took her little hand to help her feel the funny pantaloons and costume she was wearing. No one could really see them but me -- except God, perhaps -- just another reason among many that her place in Heaven was already reserved. Her Heart and Caring for connecting with Children of Any age or condition was one of her Greatest Gifts which had a powerful Influence on many lives besides mine. It inspired this Poem:

"A little hand on a pantaloon,
Seeing what eyes cannot,
Upon the knee of a special soul,
Who gives with all she's got...
Among the midst of stops and starts,
She takes the time to kneel,
And show a little hand and heart
How to see by 'feel'....
It matters not her 'cousin's' size,
Or shape in which he's born,
Behind that freckled face disguise,
She lights up those who mourn!
Through all the years I've watched her steps,
Moving many a tune,
But never a step sent such love to my heart
As that hand on the pantaloon!"

My siblings, Pat, Cindie, Jim and I inherited more than a Unique Unconventional Childhood, including an unexpected Spiritual education in a time when working women were pioneers in the work force. As her youngest 'sensitive child,' I would often sneak away and express my tender feelings in Poetry -- in between performing 'Shirley Temple' and 'Judy Garland' songs.

Mother surprised me one day with a bound booklet of many Tender Poems of my youth I had attempted to type with her help. Her Deep Faith Still gives this 'sensitive child' within me the Strength to Keep On Keepin' On, as she would say, to "Fulfill my Mission" in this world. What an Example she set for us All!

Thank You, Mother, for your pensive blue eyes becoming full, when I would give you my work to read. I pray you can 'See' this Dream Finally materializing from your Heavenly Home.

Your haunting Blue Eyes must be even more Beautiful reading them Now, reflecting from the Wings of Angels.

And we are Positive that Now "God's Hands are on your pantaloon."

"See Ya Down The Road, Cuz!"

• George Fowler ("Dance Of a Fallen Monk") and his beloved Lori --
George was a Phenomenal Author and Spiritual Teacher. Together with his precious wife Lori, they became my Angels on earth and in Heaven. Their Spiritual Mentorship and Soul Friendship Inspired and Soothed a confused young girl on her continuing Path toward Enlightenment. The hours we would discuss the Spiritual Path had a profound effect on my writing and Journey. I was so honored when my little Poem "Purify, Oh Purify" was included in his book.

PURIFY, OH, PURIFY

Sweet Angels of my Life,
Lighten Wings so meant to Fly ...
Far Above the Fright
PURIFY, OH PURIFY
Each and Every Sight --
Help me see through each I meet
The Daylight through the Night.
And as I hold to Higher Ground,
Help me Feel You Strong
To finally know Deep in my Soul --
God's Love's Where I Belong.

364

Little did I know then the Strong Influence my little "Coffee Times With George" would have to this day -- even after he left the planet:

"COFFEE-TIMES WITH GEORGE"

Tales of tears, and joys and fears --
One Lifetime seems so short,
When in one hour, such Wisdom showers
In my "Coffee Times With George."
With my Heart in Hand, in line we'd stand
waiting to sit down ...
Yet standing by, in Smiling Eyes, already Peace was found!
"Imagined Crushes" to my Heart were soothed with stories told:
Of kittens waiting to depart, 'til an old friend they behold ...
As tears well up in my "old" friend's eyes, more youthful than a colt!
My Heart swells up as I realize these precious times are Gold.
For of all the gifts this lifetime gives
with "Successes" yet to soar,
My sweetest times have been in line:
My "Coffee-Times with George."
What e'er the "Dilemma of the Day"
He has the Power to LAUGH,
Glancing looks at books and cooks, we'd jest with all the Paths.
Now, in my mind I'm still "in line," though those days of sweetness passed --
Yet remain more Real, as I still Feel his Presence that still lasts ...
Each time I hear a kitten purr, excited to explore --
It reminds of my "Spirit Talks":
My "Coffee-Times With George."

I am Grateful to still be connected to his beloved wife Lori, as she continues to Inspire the world around her. Our 'Heart to Heart' conversations are like a True Salve to my Soul. And her Inner Joy and Courage to experience Life to its Fullest at Any Age -- even on her own now -- is a contagious balm of Healing and Inspiration in this world. Lori was so kind to give me a ring George used to wear. I faithfully wear it to this day. Their sweet influence of 'Living with your Soul Mate' was so great in my life, my amazing Husband and I decided to marry on their wedding date. My 'Spiritual Godfather' and his Angel Wife Lori, will forever remain close in my Heart.

• <u>My Gifted Soul Sisters On this Journey</u>, Siblings Pat Little and Cindie Haynie have stuck by me through lots of changes in my life, and Lovingly and Patiently read many of these poems in the wee hours during the birthing of this book. And special thanks to my dear, life long friend and 'Maid of Honor,' Ayn Maddox, who grew up with me through so many 'rites of passage' I write about here. Thanks Y'all for All of your Encouragement and 'Sista Support!'

• <u>My Daddy</u> always made his little girl feel so Special to him – as he lovingly did for each of us. He always had a way of making us feel important to him, especially with the last 'surprise baby' I was (another Story in itself :-). A Sweet and Quiet man he was, who took such pride and caring for each of his children. He had so much fun sharing many of his own poems, dreams and songs with us, and would so love holding this book right now! Thank You, Daddy, for Loving us through All ....

• <u>All My Sweet Family</u>, including brother Jim, Each of my talented Nephews, Nieces, Cousins and my Mr. Prince's caring, loving Family. I am so grateful they are now a part of mine. Great Faith and Gratitude I have for you All!

• <u>My Dear Friends Along The Way</u> -- I only Wish I was able to Name All of You here. Each one of you are Profoundly Special to me. (I do think You Know Who You Are :-) You never knew the Influence you were having as I silently wrote my lessons learned in the wee hours.

• <u>Jeff Bowen</u> is my Incredibly Talented Musical Comrade from my 'Judy Garland Show' Years who stuck by me through many a creative heart tugging episode. I cherish our days of 'Musical Improv' together. His Musical Talent and Fun Sense of Humor makes him a most Unique Entertainer in this business. Ah, the show biz stories we could tell -- but then, That's Another Book!

• <u>Bob and Fred, Cindy Jean Smith, Jamie Oakman (my performing "Pointless Sister")</u> for their heartfilled kindness and caring at life changing moments in my life. Soul Thanks Rhee for Being There!

• <u>The Great Teachers on my Path</u> -- I hope they know the Creative Impact they have had on my Life's Journey. A Special Heart Thanks To Fred Rogers, Oprah Winfrey and ALL the Great Writers and Souls she has shared with the world through the years. My soul is also thankful for the Inspirational Writings of Dr. Maya Angelou, Dr. Wayne Dyer, Dr. Deepak Chopra, Eckhart Tolle, Marianne Williamson, Jack Canfield, Michael A. Singer, Gary Zukav, Brené Brown, Carolyn Myss, Byron Katie, Elizabeth Gilbert and Mike Dooley. The full list would fill another book, including so many Wonderful Spiritual Authors Louise Hay's "Hay House" has shared with the world. We All Affect Each Other More Than we know. Incredible how God speaks to us through each Encounter. I have unending Gratitude for My Soul Savior Jesus Christ, Living Deeply In my Heart. My Gratitude is Boundless and Endless!

• <u>Dolly Parton and my Dollywood Family</u> -- My Soul has been Deeply Inspired by the Unstoppable Strength and Heart of Dolly. Thank you Steve Summers for originally bringing me here! My Dollywood Family Through The Years has taught me how to Truly 'Live In The Joy of The Moment' in an often scary world. I am Forever Grateful for your Generosity Of Love, Support and Caring.

• <u>Many Thousands of Guests at Dollywood</u> have traveled with me and inspired many of these poems through the personal stories they shared with me and the numerous times we prayed together at "Miss Lillian's Wishing Well" (Page 160). You Inspired me at times you didn't even know it. We truly Are all Connected on this Journey!
• <u>Special Artistic Thanks</u> to lovely Artist Gale Littleton for her beautiful drawing accompanying my Poem "Hugs For The Holidays" (Page 321). She and her kind husband Jimmy's Spirits Bless many during Dollywood's Harvest and Gospel Celebration.

• <u>The Real Authors Of my Words</u> --
My Special Angels who have Followed, Inspired and Protected me Through Many a Dark Night Of The Soul.

• <u>My Heavenly Father and Creator</u> --
Who Truly Made ALL of Us -- and This -- Possible!

"IN 5O YEARS ...."

IN 5O YEARS WHERE WILL THESE BE,
THESE WORDS I WRITE AND SING?
IN 5O YEARS WILL I BE HERE,
OR ON SOME ANGEL'S WING?

TIME KEEPS WAKING UP MY SOUL
TO THE PASSING OF US ALL-
SO SURREAL MY CHILDHOOD GOALS,
WHEN SO QUICKLY WE CAN FALL.

LIFE COMES AND GOES SO QUICKLY HERE-
DISCONNECTING HEARTS ...
WHAT IS IT FOR? WHAT KEEPS THE DOORS
FROM KEEPING US APART?

I KNOW YOU LIVE INSIDE OF ME,
GOD SPIRIT OF THE LIGHT,
YET ON THIS EARTH OF FLESH AND DIRT,
THERE'S THE CYCLING OF THE NIGHT ...

I KNOW THE DAYLIGHT ALWAYS COMES-
IT'S NEVER STOPPED ITS FLIGHT ...
YET SOMEHOW DEEP INSIDE OF ME,
LIVES HAUNTED HUMAN FRIGHT.

HELP ME RECOGNIZE YOU HERE-
LASTING AS THINGS FADE ...
HELP ME REALIZE MY FEARS
DISAPPEAR THROUGH GRACE ...

YOUR GRACE PROTECTING EARTHLY ERRS-
ELEVATING GRAVES
THAT WE MADE WITH EARTHLY CARES,
FORGETTING YOUR EMBRACE.

THE ONLY THING THAT LASTS OUR PASTS-
AS REAL AS BREATH WE BREATHE,
IS YOUR GREAT LOVE THAT SWEETLY ASKS,
REMEMBER? YOU'RE IN ME!

About The Author

So they call her The "Chickie Spirit Lady!"

Say WHAAT?!

"What IS a 'Chickie Spirit Lady'?" -- you may ask :-)

Combine:
- The Humor of a Comic
- With the Heart of a Sensitive Spiritual Seeker
- Mix ever So Gently with Everyone's 'Child Within,'
- Bake over decades of personal experience of keeping your Center in a political and corporate show biz world of unpredictable happenings,
- And Meet Poet Connie Freeman Prince, by all accounts still calling herself a forever 'Work In Progress.'

Connie's Path To Writing was inspired while living the Unconventional Life of an Entertainer seeking Truth.

She began whistling as a baby before she constructed her first word. At the tender age of One she began appearing along with her siblings on their Mother's Live Children's TV Show, "The Cousin Tuny Show" in Jackson, TN.

Besides performing Shirley Temple Songs, Judy Garland, Marilyn Monroe, Mae West, Betty Boop, Lily Tomlin and Dolly Parton Impersonations, among others, she also performed in Radio, TV and Film, One Woman Shows, Opryland, Disney World, Herschend Family Entertainment and Cruise Ships. One of her most fun portrayals was the female lead in the Ray Stevens movie "Get Serious." She often muses about her humorous Journey To Spiritual Enlightenment: "Within One year, my 'Betty Boop' transcended Into playing the 'Virgin Mary,' and then to playing 'The Chicken Lady' Giving 'Chickie Blessings' to all the sweet guests at Dollywood! Doesn't God have an Amazing Sense Of Humor?!"

A life changing Experience of a Pituitary Tumor years ago woke her up synchronistically from abusive relationships and frightening turns of events that stopped her in her tracks. This led her to re-examine The Meaning Of it ALL.

Connie became more fascinated through her life as a Performing Artist, with just Where her Creativity came From. Always drawn to the Spiritual Meaning Behind Everything -- The Purpose of Why we are All Here -- led her to voracious Reading and Studying Of Spiritual Practices Around the world.

Her spiritual writing was profoundly affected by another life changing moment she witnessed in her youth:

"The eve of my high school graduation was spent at the Funeral Home with my family and my late cousin Carol. I'll never forget life going into slow motion as I witnessed her ominous, fragile walk up to the tiny casket of her baby son. His death from a tragic accident in her home took the breath of life out of us all. The memory of her and her family's profound grief never left me. I always related to her since she was a sensitive Poet, along with her musically gifted brother Sonny.

Shortly afterwards, when I was a theater major in college, a professor surprised me one day in an elective Creative Writing class. He asked the class to write about an experience that had a memorable influence in their life. I hesitantly wrote about that haunting moment observing this heartbroken mother at this most horrific time of her life. I sat there stunned, and the room froze as he read my composition aloud. The professor encouraged me to pursue the life of a writer, but alas, the Lights of The Stage lured me into the more 'extroverted' part of my personality (hiding the more 'Sensitive' part) for many years to come."

Writing poetry from her youth through adulthood has always been her refuge. Fast forward many decades of Loves and Losses and Joys and Heartbreaks -- and you'll find in these pages "The Poetic Guide for Sensitive Souls." Life has a way of coming Full Circle, doesn't it?

Today, Connie as "Miss Lillian" (The Chicken Lady) entertains hundreds of thousands of beloved Dollywood guests each year, performing 'Comedic Spirit Improv' on her Little Banjolele and Ukuleles. Her 'Musical Poetry' is Always In Progress.'

Her quiet times of re-charging and renewal are spent in Peaceful Bliss in The Foothills Of The Smoky Mountains, with her fur family of Rescue Cats and Critters, along with her Beloved Soul Mate Muse Husband "Mr. Prince" (Another Love Story in Itself!). Their Smoky Mountain Home was the Backdrop in creating many of the Poems you are now holding.

She and her Beloved Husband and Writing Partner, Bobby Prince (Composer, Sound Designer and Lifetime Achievement Award Winner In The Video Game Industry), have also composed the Inspiring Children's Book With Songs, "Elvin The Tiniest Elf."

ElvinTheTiniestElf.com

More Songs, Poems and Creative Adventures always in Progress!!

"A Life in Rhyme -
These Evolving Times.
May It Inspire Yours
With Smiles that Shine!"

Connie and her "Prince Charming"

Take time to laugh... it is the music of the soul!

Goldfab

*Connie as "Miss Lillian" (The Chicken Lady) at Dollywood
with her Mr. Prince and her faithful companion "Chicken Little, Jr."
Chickie Spirit Blessings!*

"Miss Lillian"
(The Chicken Lady)
At Dollywood

 MissLillianTheChickenLady

 chickspiritlady

 @chickspiritlady

 MissLillianDollywood

Email: MissLillian@ChickenLady.biz

 FACEBOOK

 INSTAGRAM

 TWITTER

 YOUTUBE -
MISS LILLIAN

 YOUTUBE -
CHICKINSPIRATION

Special "Logo" Gift Thanks to my Wonderful Friend Lon Smart,
Creative Concept Artist/Character Illustrator from Disney World.

Made in the USA
Columbia, SC
17 November 2021

49165473R00215